"I am Ninja...
My Way is Ninjutsu"

— Tiger Scroll of the Koga Ninja

Ninja

The Shadow Warrior

Ninja

The Shadow Warrior

Joel Levy

STERLING

New York / London
www.sterlingpublishing.com

Library of Congress Cataloging-in-Publication Data Available

1 2 3 4 5 6 7 8 9 10

Published in 2008 by Sterling Publishing Co., Inc.
387 Park Avenue South, New York, NY 10016

© 2007 JW Cappelens forlag under license from Gusto Company AS
Written by Joel Levy
Original concept by Gusto Company
Designed by Allen Boe
Illustrations: Miguel Coimbra, AnnDréa Boe, and public domain

Distributed in Canada by Sterling Publishing
c/o Canadian Manda Group, 165 Dufferin Street
Toronto, Ontario, Canada M6K 3h6

For information about custom editions, special sales, premium and corporate purchases,
please contact Sterling Special Sales Department at 800-805-5489 or specialsales@
sterlingpub.com

Manufactured in China

Sterling ISBN: 978-1-4027-6313-7

Contents

Introduction

"I AM NINJA

My Magic is Training . . .

My Body is Control . . .

My Strength is Adaptability . . .

My Weapons are Everything That Exists . . .

MY WAY IS NINJUTSU"

Extract from the Ninja's Covenant,
from Jay Sensei's *Tiger Scroll of the Koga Ninja*

Mention the word "ninja" to anyone, in the East or West, and they will probably picture a black-garbed super-assassin with stealth skills and martial arts prowess. In Japan, the popular conception is more highly developed, with the ninja as a folk hero possessing supernatural powers, including invisibility and flight. What are the origins of this extraordinary and enthralling character? Is the popular picture accurate? What do we know about the history and lore of the ninja, and the secrets of his craft? This book explores the answers to all these questions—from the birth of the ninja and their history, to the amazing tools, tactics, and techniques of the ninja way, *ninjutsu*, to their place in popular culture.

NINJA VERSUS SHINOBI NO MONO

Any examination of the world of the ninja must begin with an explanation of the origins of the word "ninja," because the etymology of the word points to its essence. The word "ninja" comes from two kanji characters that can be read in two different ways. Kanji is a form of Japanese writing that uses pictograms derived from Chinese. Kanji characters effectively allow two languages to be written at once—a character can be read as a native Japanese word or a Chinese-derived word.

In the Chinese-derived pronunciation, the characters are read as *nin* and *sha*, giving the compound word "ninja." In the Japanese pronunciation, they give the words *shinobi* and *mono* which, when put together, imply a linking word, *no*, so that they read *shinobi no mono*. Both *nin* and *shinobi* have the same meaning: "stealth," or "quiet action," but also "to endure." Meanwhile, *sha* and *mono* both mean "person." Both ways of reading the kanji characters translate as much the same thing: "a person skilled in the art of stealth," or "one who endures." Many translations from Japanese sources use the words *shinobi* or *shinobi no mono* interchangeably with the word "ninja," but in the West the shorter, easier term is the one that caught on. A common modern translation of "ninja" is "shadow warrior," which, while not technically accurate, certainly captures the spirit of the original characters.

忍者

"Ninjutsu" is the collective term for the skills and techniques practiced by the ninja. Like "ninja," it is a compound word, combining the *nin* character with the *jutsu* character, meaning "skill" or "technique." The word "ninjutsu" also encompasses the philosophy and culture of the ninja, including their way of life and social organization. Full *ninjutsu* training extends far beyond martial arts to include survival skills, meteorology, geography, psychology, acting, and philosophy. Training also encompasses the finer points of espionage, including the tactics and strategy of using these points in war. While the popular modern image of the ninja is that of an assassin, historically the ninja were much more likely to serve as spies, scouts, and commando-type covert operations forces. In some historical sources, the word "ninja" is not used; rather, individuals with ninja qualities are referred to as *kancho* (spies), *teisatsu* (scouts), *kisho* (surprise attackers), or *koran* (agitators).

NINJA VERSUS SAMURAI

Some teachers of *ninjutsu* emphasize that the key to ninja philosophy is found in the interpretation of the word "ninja" as "one who endures." In other words, the ninja philosophy is one of stoicism, of taking all that life throws at a person, enduring it, and attaining one's goal. This emphasis on the end rather than the means is part of what sets the ninja in opposition to the samurai. The samurai, who were Japan's warrior caste, developed very strict ethical and behavioral precepts that governed how they lived, fought, and died. Honor was paramount, and to maintain that honor it was essential to fight in a noble, forthright fashion: the warrior met the enemy head-on, ideally in single combat out in the open, and announced himself, actively seeking as much attention as possible, before combat. The samurai was expected to place honor above life, so that if he lost a battle, was captured, or failed in his duty to his lord ideally he committed ritual suicide.

The tradition and philosophy of the ninja were the antithesis of the samurai way. The ninja's roots were in poor farming communities and social strata that were looked down upon by the haughty and aristocratic samurai. His philosophy was to avoid open combat where possible, to use any means of subterfuge, dishonesty, trickery, or strategy to achieve his ends, and to succeed at all costs. The ninja often worked as a mercenary, with no loyalty to his employer, and was probably despised by the samurai as embodying all the traits and behaviors samurai sought to avoid.

According to Stephen Hayes, one of the leading Western proponents of *ninjutsu*, "What went on to become a highly systematic method of combat and espionage began as a shadowy counter-culture, a reaction against the mainstream of Japanese political and social tradition." This idea of the ninja as an "anti-samurai" is a vital element in the modern discourse about ninja.

忍者

Timeline

10,000 B.C. – A.D. 538	Jomon Period; hunter-gatherer culture
300 B.C. – A.D. 300	Yayoi Period; distinguished by rice cultivation
A.D. 300 – A.D. 700	Kofun Period; weaponry and metalworking
512	Approximate date that Sun Tzu publishes *The Art of War*
710	Japan's first capital city at Nara
794	Capital moves to Kyoto
796	Title of *Sei-i-tai* shogun introduced
907	End of Tang Dynasty in China; Chinese refugees flee to Japan's Iga and Koga regions
1156	Hogen Rebellion
1184	Togakure Daisuke flees to the mountains of Iga Province and meets Kasumi Gakure
1185	Gempei War ends
1185–89	Minamoto Yoshitsune becomes a ninja-like fugitive

1192	Shogunate created by Minamoto Yoritomo
1274	First Mongol invasion of Japan
1281	Second Mongol invasion of Japan
1330s	Killing of Himma Saburo: the first ninja assassination
1336	Battle of Minatogawa; start of Nanbokucho Wars
1348	Battle of Shijo Nawate
1467	Onin War begins
1477	Onin War ends
1541	Hattori Hanzo born
1543	Arrival of Europeans in Japan
1560	Imagawa Yoshimoto marches on Kyoto, but is defeated by Oda Nobunaga
1562	Siege of Sawayama Castle; siege of Kaminojo Castle
1579	Iga Suppression under Oda Nobunaga
1581	Battle of Ukishimagahara; dispersal of Iga *ryu*
1582	Oda Nobunaga murdered
1590	Tokugawa Ieyasu marches into Edo, accompanied by Iga ninja; Hattori Hanzo dies

1592	First invasion of Korea
1596	Hattori Hanzo dies
1597	Second invasion of Korea
1600	Siege of Hataya Castle
1603	Era of Warring States ends with reunification of Japan; Tokugawa shogunate established at Edo (Tokyo)
1605	Band of Iga ninja revolt and split into four factions
1614–15	Siege of Osaka Castle
1637–38	Shimabara Rebellion
1702	The Forty-seven Ronin of Ako kill Kira Yoshinaka
1802	First known image of a classic black-clad ninja
1853	Final ninja mission recorded: Sawamura Yasusuke attempts to infiltrate "black ships" under command of Commodore Perry
1864–68	Meiji Restoration
1867	Shogunate officially ends
1868	Edo renamed Tokyo and replaces Kyoto as the official capital (even though Edo had been the de facto capital since 1603)

忍 者

The reputation
of a thousand
years may be
determined
by the conduct
of one hour.

—*Japanese Proverb*

Togakure-ryu, traces its origins back to Togakure Daisuke, a minor samurai in the service of a defeated lord who ...ed to the mountains of Iga Province in 1184. Here he encountered a Taoist monk, variously known as Kain Doshi or Kasumi Gakure (which loosely means "hiding in the mist"), who trained him in the techniques that would form the basis of the ninjutsu ryu founded by his descendants.

Chapter 1

History of the Ninja

The history of the ninja is sketchy at best, for they rarely appear as full-fledged "actors" on the stage of history. Instead, like the black-clad prop-handlers of Kabuki theater from whom some elements of the ninja mythology may derive (see page 57), the ninja exist mainly on the fringe of history, occasionally popping up in the midst of the action, yet remaining enigmatically veiled.

ROOTS OF THE NINJA

There is a distinction between the use of *shinobi* methods by conventional troops and commanders and a full-fledged secret brotherhood or caste of specifically initiated ninja. Early in ninja history, there was no formal organization of the ninja or concept of *ninjutsu*. Only later did ninja methods became organized into *ryu*, which usually translates as "school" (as in a tradition of training) but which might more properly be interpreted as "clan" in the case of ninja.

Masaaki Hatsumi, an eminent modern teacher and promoter of *ninjutsu*, claims that "The history of the ninja is
long and ancient. Some say it extends back for over 2,500
years, but in fact there are records going back as far as
4,300 years." The basis for this claim is unclear, but he
establishes that he is referring mainly to the basic skills of
stealth, resourcefulness, and adaptability that characterize
ninjutsu. In other words, the basics of *shinobi* would have
been developed since earlier times, and in Japanese folklore these skills are linked to legendary characters, such
as the eighth century Prince Yamato, or to mythical crea-
tures, such as the *tengu*—fierce bird-man demons skilled
in swordplay and warrior ways. Such figures constitute the
mythical origins of the ninja.

THE CHINESE INFLUENCE

More realistically, the seeds of *ninjutsu* are probably
derived from the impact of Chinese invaders on Japanese
culture. Martial arts writer Jay Sensei traces the roots of
Japanese martial arts, including *ninjutsu*, to sixth-century
China, which had derived them in turn from the South
Asian Buddhist priests who had first developed the arts of
body conditioning and the use of medicines and potions.
These arts, specifically those involving espionage and covert operations, were first brought to Japan, he suggests, by
Chinese pirates who staged raids on the Japanese islands
and used advance-guards of ninja-style commando troops
to spread fear and panic.

More conventionally, the Chinese influence is ascribed to refugees fleeing the chaos that attended the collapse of the Tang Dynasty in China in the early tenth century. Generals and sages alike made the crossing to Japan and, according to legend, found refuge in the mountains of the Iga and Koga areas, the traditional ninja heartland. There, they supposedly combined their esoteric spiritual and physical systems with martial arts and military training to create *ninjutsu*, which was subsequently passed on to the locals.

Stephen Turnbull, a leading historian of Japanese warrior castes, points to an earlier Chinese influence. Sun Tzu, the great Chinese military theorist, who is believed to have lived in the sixth century B.C., wrote extensively on what might be called *shinobi* techniques and strategies in his famous book *The Art of War*. For instance, he advocated the extensive use of spies and covert and psychological warfare, laying down a blueprint for what would become staple elements of *ninjutsu*. Sun Tzu first became known in Japan in the eighth century A.D., and Turnbull traces the start of ninja activity to the influence of his writings.

The final piece in the puzzle of ninja origins may be found in early stories featuring ninja-like characters that often involve bandits and outlaws of the Robin Hood type. Perhaps, clans of bandits and brigands in parts of Japan where the writ of centralized, samurai-led control did not take hold—areas such as the mountainous Iga and Koga provinces—developed *shinobi* methods out of necessity, and evolved later into full-fledged ninja.

JAPAN

Koga Province

•Edo

Kyoto•

Iga Province

Ōsaka

THE NINJA HEARTLAND

From at least the twelfth century onwards, the use of *shinobi* methods was a well-established part of warfare, and when Japan was gripped by civil wars, including the Gempei War (in the late twelfth century A.D.) and later the Nanbokucho War (in the mid-fourteenth century A.D.), units and troops whose description match that of the ninja start to receive elliptical and passing mentions. Accounts of these wars speak of spies and attempted assassinations, covert operations against heavily fortified castles, and clever ruses and stratagems on the battlefield.

BIRTH OF THE RYU

This is also the time when, scholars claim, the formal *ryu* of *ninjutsu* came into being. Many of the *ryu* have legendary or semi-legendary foundation stories, such as the tale of Minamoto Yoshitsune, brother of a powerful samurai who later became shogun (military dictator of Japan). Yoshitsune fell out with his brother and, from A.D. 1185 to 1189 was a fugitive, during which time legend attributes to him a colorful career as a ninja-like outlaw with many adventures. Yoshitsune is credited with having founded the Yoshitsune-*ryu* of *ninjutsu*.

The best known *ninjutsu ryu* today, the Togakure-*ryu*, traces its origins back to Togakure Daisuke, a minor samurai in the service of a defeated lord who fled to the mountains of Iga Province in 1184. Here he encountered a Taoist monk, variously known as Kain Doshi or Kasumi Gakure (which translates as "hiding in the mist"), who trained him in the techniques that would form the basis of the *ninjutsu ryu* founded by his descendants.

The number of *ryu* founded during and after this period is disputed, but Masaaki Hatsumi, the leading authority on *ninjutsu*, quotes the figure seventy, while other sources claim there were more than two hundred. Most of these *ryu* were centered in the mountainous provinces of Iga and Koga, where the Iga-*ryu* and the Koga-*ryu* were said to have nearly fifty sub-schools each.

IGA AND KOGA—LANDSCAPE AND LIVELIHOOD

Iga and Koga are neighboring provinces in south central Honshu, the main island of Japan. Despite their central position, their mountainous terrain left the area remote from mainstream Japanese society and politics. Iga in particular is a collection of high valleys ringed by rugged mountains that has been likened to Switzerland in terms of both its geography and the resulting social and political character of the area: independent, egalitarian, and doughty. These characteristics produced hardy warriors who had little or no allegiance to feudal overlords, and who were thus able to hire themselves out as mercenaries. When the *shinobi* techniques of *ninjutsu* were added to the mix, the result was a ninja culture, in which small farming communities supported yeoman-warriors who could just as readily wield a sword as a scythe.

GOLDEN AGE OF THE NINJA

With the establishment of the ninja *ryu* and the widespread acceptance of the value of *shinobi* methods on the battlefield, the stage was set for the ninja to become major players in warfare, particularly when the brutal Onin War triggered a long period of civil war known as the Sengoku Jidai, or Period of Warring States. For nearly three hundred years up until the mid-fifteenth century, Japan had mostly fallen into line behind a succession of powerful shoguns, but increasing economic problems, coupled with a weak shogunate, led to an armed dispute getting out of hand and becoming the Onin War (1467–1477). This in turn fatally undermined the authority of the shogun, leading to a power vacuum and resulting in a free-for-all, as provincial governors and warlords grabbed local power and set themselves up as *daimyo* (feudal lords). For the next 133 years, these *daimyo* would vie with each other for dominance until the country was united once more under a powerful and stable shogunate.

With more than a century of warfare—characterized mainly by the construction and siege of great castles and the exploits of the *daimyo*—there was a definite need for the services of the ninja. Many of the tasks that had to be undertaken for a *daimyo* to wage war successfully were distasteful, dishonorable, or simply too difficult for his samurai, so he would hire ninja instead.

There was also a degree of cross-over between ninja warriors and special cadres of troops trained in *shinobi* techniques by individual *daimyo*. Examples of the latter include the *mitsumono* warriors of Takeda Shingen, who were low-caste soldiers trained in techniques of espionage, reconnaissance, and scouting; and the *nokizaru* (rooftop monkeys) of Uesugi Kenshin, named for their prowess at getting into strongholds via the roof.

CASTLE COMMANDOS

It was during this period of political and military unrest that the classic pattern of ninja activity was set, in particular the role of the ninja as castle infiltrators. The typical Japanese castle was a formidable fortification atop a hill, surrounded by a moat and protected by high stone base-walls surmounted by plastered wattle-and-daub and/or timber walls, with multiple baileys (defensive rings) and keeps. For a samurai, any approach short of a carefully announced full-frontal assault was dishonorable. The ninja, however, were incredibly skilled at infiltrating a castle without being noticed, taking up positions inside, reconnoitering and gathering intelligence, and, if called into action, spreading destruction, panic, and discord by setting fires, dispatching guards, and attacking the defenders while dressed in the same armor as them.

Such actions tended to be recorded somewhat laconically in chronicles of the times. For instance, according to the diary of Buddhist Abbot Eishun of Tamon-In, written in

1541 and quoted in Stephen Turnbull's *Ninja: The True Story of Japan's Secret Warrior Cult,* "The units from Iga province entered Kasagi Castle in secret and set fire to a few of the priest's quarters. They also set fire to outbuildings in various places in the third bailey. They captured the first and second baileys." The lord of the castle, Kizawa Nagamasa, was mortally wounded (possibly by a ninja?) and the castle soon fell to its attackers. A more effusive account of a ninja exploit comes from a chronicle called the *Ou Eikei Gunki,* which relates that during the siege of Hataya Castle in 1600 one of the defenders—"a glorious *shinobi* whose skill was renowned"—infiltrated the camp of the besieging army and stole a samurai's personal standard, which he then displayed from the castle ramparts, much to the defenders' delight and the besiegers' chagrin.

THE IGA SUPPRESSION

It was in this era that the ninja of Iga enjoyed their most rewarding period of employment, but in 1581 they fell afoul of the most powerful *daimyo* in Japan, Oda Nobunaga. The men of Iga had aroused the enmity of Nobunaga's son in an earlier campaign, and in 1579 he launched two attempts to conquer the territory and suppress the ninja *ryu,* both of which were thwarted by the Iga ninja, who used their skills to wage guerrilla warfare against numerically superior forces. Two years later, Nobunaga himself took charge of a third attempt, sending over 44,000 men into Iga in a multi-pronged blitz attack from all directions. According to one estimate, a mere 4,000 ninja stood in opposition to this force. Despite valiant resistance (which included an assassination attempt on Nobunaga involving hidden snipers and a cannon), the Iga *ryu* were suppressed and the survivors scattered to other parts of the country, where they found refuge and set up new *ryu*.

THE SHOGUN'S NINJA

One destination for fugitive Iga ninja was the Mikawa province, home of Tokugawa Ieyasu. At this point, Ieyasu was a minor but respected *daimyo*; an ally of Nobunaga but one with close links to the Koga and Iga ninja. In earlier times, the Koga ninja had helped him to capture an enemy castle and secure hostages, while at the time of the Iga suppression he counted among his chief retainers Hattori "Devil" Hanzo, a warrior from Iga who has since become renowned as one of the most famous ninja of all time. Ieyasu's association with the ninja was to pay off for both sides.

In 1582, just a year after his attack on Iga, Oda Nobunaga was murdered by one of his own generals, rendering vulnerable those who had previously been in his camp. Tokugawa Ieyasu found himself in particular danger because he was away from home at the time, and faced a perilous road back to the relative safety of Tokugawa territory. Fortunately for Ieyasu, he had with him Devil Hanzo, who went ahead and scouted out an alternative route back through

Iga country. Normally this would carry its own hazards of brigands and bandits, but with Hanzo's contacts and the good will he had secured by offering refuge to the Iga ninja the previous year, Ieyasu was able to secure safe passage home.

Over the next twenty years, with Hanzo and units of ninja at his side, Ieyasu's star rose. When Ieyasu marched into Edo (modern Tokyo) in 1590 to establish it as his new capital, the Iga ninja were at his side. Recognizing their value, he appointed them his personal bodyguards. The Iga ninja under Hanzo were quartered outside the western gates of the castle in Edo, and the area itself became known as Hanzo-cho, while the western gate of Edo Castle was named the Hanzo Mon gate.

In one incident in 1600, the Koga ninja again came to Ieyasu's aid, perpetrating a classic *ninjutsu* ruse to help him escape a difficult situation. The powerful *daimyo*, on the verge of achieving ultimate victory, was threatened with a potentially lethal ambush, so his ninja guard created a dummy replica of their lord, filled it with explosives, and set it atop the Tokugawa carriage, which they escorted as if nothing were amiss. When the enemies attacked, the gunpowder was set off, killing the Koga ninja escort but also the ambushers, giving the carriage carrying the real Ieyasu precious time to escape. In recognition of this and other acts of service, a band of Koga ninja were assigned to the defense of the front gate of Edo castle. Later, under

the third Tokugawa shogun, Iemitsu, this system of ninja guards was formalized under the title *akeyashykiban*, a protocol that governed how the castle was to be defended when the shogun and his personal bodyguard were absent.

Finally, in 1602, Ieyasu became undisputed shogun of a reunited Japan, bringing an end to the Period of Warring States and ushering in the 260-year dynasty known as the Tokugawa Shogunate.

DECLINE OF THE NINJA

The end of warfare and strife also meant the end of boom time for mercenary ninja. From this period on, the ninja receded as active participants in the history of Japan. The most historically "visible" ninja continued to be the Iga and Koga men, 300 of whom had been taken into the service of the shogun Tokugawa Ieyasu. Meanwhile, some of those ninja who remained independent resorted to banditry, with many becoming popular folk heroes.

THE BAND OF IGA

The ninja who had been taken into Ieyasu's service, originally under the leadership of Hattori "Devil" Hanzo, came to be known as the Band of Iga. When Devil Hanzo died in 1596 (see page 161), he was succeeded by his son, who bore the same name but shared few of his qualities. Hanzo's son was not fully trained in *ninjutsu*, and his style of leadership was unpopular. In 1605, the Band of Iga revolted, declaring Hanzo's son unworthy of his name. They barricaded themselves in a temple, threatening to execute him and take their own lives if their demands for change were not met. Hanzo's son was dismissed and the Band split into four factions, each under the command of a relatively low-ranking samurai. Already their prestige was on the wane.

THE SIEGE OF OSAKA CASTLE

However, the Band of Iga did play an important part in helping Ieyasu during the Siege of Osaka Castle (also known as the Winter and Summer Campaigns), a major threat to his authority that erupted in 1614–1615. Ieyasu had come to prominence by supplanting the family that originally succeeded Nobunaga, the Toyotomi clan. When a scion of the clan, Toyotomi Hideyori, started to gather an army around its power base at Osaka, Ieyasu launched a series of campaigns against him that culminated in some of the largest battles ever seen on the Japanese mainland.

Ieyasu's ninja cohorts were employed in espionage and covert operations, and many credit them with swinging the campaign in the shogun's favor. Some were dressed as ronin, unaffiliated samurai looking for work, and sent to infiltrate the Osaka Castle defenders. Here, they gathered intelligence and helped to sow discord in classic ninja fashion, including spreading disinformation that loyal members of the garrison were part of a spy ring. Following the *ninjutsu* approach to espionage (see Chapter 4, page 126), Ieyasu also used captured Toyotomi ninja as double agents, either turning them to his side or feeding them false information and allowing them to escape. In one particular incident, the ninja used their skill at passing messages by arrow to target a dangerous Toyotomi general,

Sanada Yukimura, who was renowned for his bravery and tactical acumen. They were able to fire a note from Ieyasu into Yukimura's specific area of the castle, offering him a hefty bribe to change sides.

THE SHOGUN'S SECRET SERVICE

With a mainly unbroken peace across the land, there was little call for the services of the ninja, and those in the service of the shogunate increasingly found their status diminishing. Their main role changed from warrior elite to a sort of secret police, used by the Tokugawa shogunate as an instrument of authoritarian rule and a tool for the ruthless suppression of all dissent. In this role they were called by various names, including *oniwaban*, which literally translates as "one in the garden," but more accurately means "honor-garden-guard," possibly relating to where they were stationed at the palace. Jay Sensei suggests it was a term of ridicule more properly translated as "gardener," reflecting the derision aimed at the declining ninja by the snobbish court samurai and ladies-in-waiting, who saw them as little more than glorified servants.

During the reign of the eighth Tokugawa shogun, Tokugawa Yoshimune, the *oniwaban* were organized into a formal cadre known as the Oniwabanshu, who, according to legend, roamed as far afield as America in the secret service of the Shogunate. Another title was *onmitsu* (spy, or detective). The *oniwaban* had a less-than-enviable job—practitioners were looked down upon as dishonorable, and were not af-forded official status or recognition, having to travel and col-lect intelligence incognito. Possibly the lowest point was reached with the introduction of *kobushikata*—small gangs made up of ten agents working undercover as manual laborers and under Iga ninja supervisors. Laboring on the roads gave them a good excuse to move around and observe the locals unremarked, but it could not have been glamorous work.

THE END OF THE NINJA

With their status declining, and with the passing away of the older generation of ninja along with their store of knowledge, fewer young men prepared to undergo the necessary arduous training, and the number of ninja dwindled. Indeed, their days as warriors did not long survive the start of the Edo period. A group of veteran ninja were sent on a mission to help suppress the Christian peasants' revolt of the Shimabara Rebellion of 1637–1638, but they met with limited success, and were never featured in battle again.

According to Stephen Hayes, the final record of a ninja mission dates to 1853, when the ninja Sawamura Yasusuke (or Sawamura Jinzaburo, depending on the source) was sent to infiltrate one of the recently arrived "black ships" of Commodore Perry, the American naval commander who had been sent to pry open the Japanese markets to Western influence via gunboat diplomacy. Yasusuke's task

was to collect intelligence on the foreign newcomers, and Hayes says that, "to this day, the Sawamura family archives in Mie Prefecture's Iga-Ueno City still contain the two documents purloined by their stealthy ancestor—two letters containing a Dutch sailor song extolling the delights of French women in bed and British women in the kitchen."

THE SECRET TORCH

This would indeed be an undignified end to the ninja story except that, according to modern *ninjutsu* practitioners, a dedicated core of ninja masters carefully preserved their art and passed the torch of *ninjutsu* through secret writings, such as the *Tora no Maki* (*Tiger Scrolls*) and through the teachings of the Togakure-*ryu*. Deep in the mountains of Iga, the Togakure clan transmitted their *ninjutsu* teachings from father to son and from master to pupil, eventually handing them on to the Toda family. Late in the nineteenth century, these secrets were entrusted to Takamatsu Toshitsugu, who became the thirty-third Grandmaster of the Togakure-*ryu*, and who in turn passed them on to Masaaki Hatsumi, the thirty-fourth Grandmaster. Through Hatsumi, *ninjutsu* was finally made public and its doctrine and teachings were spread throughout Japan and now across the world. Hatsumi became a major media figure, advising on and even appearing in numerous films and television series about ninja (see page 180), as well as teaching his art to disciples from the East and West, many of whom have gone on to set up their own schools in America and elsewhere.

忍 者

A single arrow is easily broken, but not ten in a bundle.

—*Japanese Proverb*

Equipment with the key characteristics of adaptability, portability, and concealability. Ninja had to move quickly and quietly, and be able to perform multiple functions in the course of a single mission, from hiding, sneaking, and remaining immobile, to climbing, running, jumping, swimming, and fighting

Chapter 2
Ninja Equipment

A central element of the ninja approach to warfare is to make full use of any objects at hand. The true ninja was incredibly resourceful and adaptable, and could use virtually anything in his vicinity to his advantage or as a weapon. He also was prepared for all eventualities and was able to use an amazing variety of often highly sophisticated gear.

Low-tech equipment with the key characteristics of adaptability, portability, and concealability encapsulates the ninja philosophy. Ninja had to move quickly and quietly, and be able to perform multiple functions in the course of a single mission—from hiding, sneaking, and remaining immobile, to climbing, running, jumping, swimming, and fighting. They often had to pass through searches and checkpoints wearing a disguise. They were only able to take on a mission what they could carry themselves. All these factors limited the amount of equipment they could take, so they tended to favor items that could be adapted for multiple purposes.

SHINOBIFUKU—THE NINJA OUTFIT

The defining characteristic of the stereotypical ninja is his black outfit with hood and face mask. In reality the *shinobifuku*, or "secret costume" of the ninja, was not necessarily black. The classic ninja *shinobifuku* consisted of a shirt with close-fitting sleeves and a jacket similar to that used today for martial arts, tucked into knee-length trousers with cloth gaiters wound around the calves. A cowl would be wrapped around the head, leaving only the face or eyes visible. The costume allowed full and easy movement while minimizing the ninja's profile by reducing the chances of light reflecting off any uncovered skin, and muffling sounds. This eliminated trailing hems, cuffs, or ties that could snag on surfaces.

This clothing was more complex than it appeared. The trousers, for instance, might have special compartments built into them for storing waste, so that a ninja hiding within an enemy's house could perform bodily functions without leaving revealing evidence. The cloth of the trousers and other parts of the outfit could serve multiple purposes, including as a flotation device (by whipping the cloth over the head and then into the water to trap air) or as a tent or a hammock when camping. Trousers might be reversible, and be colored differently on opposite sides to enhance camouflage in different environments (e.g., green for forest maneuvers and white for snowy landscapes). The *zukin*, or cowl, was often soaked with a special antiseptic

resin to make an effective bandage, or used as a filter to help purify dirty water for drinking when on the move.

Japanese warriors traditionally carried a towel that could also be used as a bandage or sling—ninja were no exception, and they carried a *sanjaku tenugui*, or "three-foot towel." An *amegasa*, or sedge hat, was commonly listed as one of the core items of ninja kit—such a hat would be useful when traveling in the rainy season, and could also help to disguise a ninja's identity and make it easier for him to pass as a harmless peasant. Authorities claim that ninja sometimes wore *yoroi* (armor), particularly light-weight armor made from thin metal plates stitched onto a cloth, skirted jacket, and hood, which could fit under normal clothes.

FOOTWEAR

Ninja wore traditional two-toed *tabi*, sock-shoes with a gap between the big toe and the rest of the toes, together with *waraji*, or straw sandals, of similar design. These might be equipped with spikes on the bottom, like shoes worn by modern sprinters for track and field, to help with traction and climbing. The sandals might also have odd-shaped soles to leave confusing tracks and throw off pursuers: the soles might be shaped like animal prints, clubfeet, or the feet of an old, lame, or fat person. They might even be "reversed," to leave tracks that appeared to point the wrong way. Although these prints would not fool an experienced tracker, they might gain the pursued ninja a few valuable moments.

UTILITY BELT

A ninja also wore a utility belt that held a variety of objects. Tied to the sash around his waist would be the *uchi-take* (also known as a *tsukedake*), a bamboo tube used as a waterproof container for gunpowder, metal shavings, and pepper (a mix for blinding opponents, like modern pepper spray), as well as tinderbox materials. Alongside it might be the *inro*, or medicine carrier, a lacquered box with various compartments for storing herbs, potions, poisons, and other ingredients. There might also be a *seki hitsu*, or "stone brush," a kind of writing kit with a slate pencil that could be used to make notes for intelligence-gathering purposes or to leave signs on rock or wood for other ninja; in an emergency it could even be thrown like a *shuriken* (see page 61). Possibly also on the belt, or alternatively over the shoulder, was the coiled *kaginawa*, or hooked rope, a length of rope with a grappling hook on one end for climbing, but which could also be used as a weapon for dragging people off their feet, and in particular for dragging soldiers off high walls.

BLACK OUT

For nighttime operations, such as castle infiltration, black was likely the best color for the *shinobifuku*. (According to Masaaki Hatsumi, even when the outfit was black, the true color was black with a reddish tinge, so that bloodstains from injuries would not show.) However, the *shinobifuku* was not always black. It could be colored for

camouflage purposes, or made to look like normal, non-military clothing for travel or while operating in costume.

Where does the image of the black-clad ninja assassin, popular since the early nineteenth century, come from from? Several theorists point to the influence of the Kabuki theatre. In Kabuki, and particularly in the related *bunraku* (puppet theatre), *kurogo* (prop-handlers) moved about the stage concurrent with the action to help produce special effects. Although they were in plain view and mingled with the actors, they wore tight-fitting black outfits that covered every part of them except a narrow slit for their eyes. This helped reduce their visual impact, and also signified to the audience that they "weren't there"—in other words, the outfit became a short-hand for invisibility, and to audiences practiced in watching Kabuki such an identification became second nature. Later in Kabuki theater ninja-like characters appeared, sometimes with magical powers of invisibility. To represent them it was natural to adapt the prop-handler's costume, which thus became the official costume of fictional ninja.

Ninja Weapons

As with the rest of ninja equipment, ninja weapons had to be light, portable, concealable, and multi-purpose in their uses: few of the weapons were used simply for fighting. A ninja would probably not carry all the weapons described here. If he was traveling or working in disguise, he might be limited to just the bare minimum of concealed weaponry, such as the *shinobijo*, or secret cane. This was a staff of bamboo, approximately three segments long, with a hollow segment at one end for carrying poison-tipped darts and a fold-out penknife-style blade in the other end.

Secret Sword

The basic ninja sword, or *katana*, was a medium-length blade. Since it was used by the ninja, or *shinobi no mono*, it was also known as a *shinobigatana* (indeed many items in the ninja inventory carry the prefix *shinobi*). The blade was typically about twenty inches long and slightly shorter than the samurai version, allowing for easier use in confined spaces and making it easier to carry. Also, for increased mobility, it was worn on the back with the hilt over the right shoulder, and was drawn with the right hand.

Apart from the blade, the other parts of the sword were also important. There was the *tsuba*, or guard, which was large and square; the *saya*, or scabbard, sometimes with a detachable tip; and the *sageo*, or cord, a twelve-inch length of strong cord attached to the scabbard. With these special parts, the sword could be used in five ways in addition to fighting:

1. **For climbing:** A classic ninja trick was to lean the sword, hilt up, against a wall, and use the *tsuba* as a step to launch oneself up and over. The sword would then be pulled up via the *sageo*, which was tied around the ankle.

2. **For combat with multiple assailants:** The sword and scabbard could be whirled around in a circle while being held by the *sageo*, thus increasing the ninja's reach and allowing him to fight off multiple opponents at once, if only for a few seconds.

3. **As a probe:** The ninja could use the sword as a probe for exploring ahead while moving about in darkness by drawing the sword almost all the way out of the scabbard, and then balancing the *saya* on the tip of the sword, while holding it in place by gripping the *sageo* in his teeth. If he encountered a guard, he could simply let go of the *sageo*, so that the *saya* would drop to the floor, and then lunge forward with the naked blade.

4. **As a launching device:** There was enough space at the bottom of the *saya* for storing a blinding combination of metal shavings, pepper, and sand. If the *saya* was gripped in

one hand and the hilt of the sword in the other, and then the former was swung out as the sword was pulled, this mix could be launched into the opponent's eyes, blinding him long enough to make the fatal strike.

5. As a tube: The detachable tip of the *saya* could be removed to allow it to be used as a blowpipe or snorkel.

The *sageo* was also useful as a multi-purpose rope for tying up opponents, making camp, laying a trip-wire, or binding wounds.

SHURIKEN

Perhaps the best-known ninja weapon is the *shuriken*. Today, this is popularly taken to mean a throwing star, which is to say a star-shaped projectile that is spun at a target. In fact, *shuriken* means "hand-hidden blade" or "behind-hand knife," and was originally a simple, small blade that could be concealed in the hand and thrown, or rather flicked, with a quick motion to distract, delay, blind, kill, or poison (if the blade was poison-tipped).

According to one source, there were over 350 different types of *shuriken*, from the original, needle-like six-inch long blades to modern complex shapes. Some two-dimensional shapes include the *juji*, or cross; the *manji*, or swastika; the *happo*, or star; the *sampo*, or triangle; and the *tatamijuji*, or folding cross, which has swiveling blades that unfold from a two-pointed shape to a four-pointed shape.

CALTROPS

Shuriken also come in three-dimensional shapes that can be used as caltrops (tetrahedral pointed devices that always have one point aiming upwards, and can be used to wound the feet of horses or warriors). These were known as *arare* (hailstones), and included: *joarare*, which are large and were used to spread fire by making bits of flaming cloth stick to doors and roofs; *chuarare*, medium-sized ones thrown at enemies; and *kaoarare*, small ones used as caltrops.

OTHER PROJECTILES

Other long-range weapons in the ninja armory included the *taibumi* (travel bow), a collapsible bow that was hinged and could be folded into a walking stick to avoid detection. Alternatively, a ninja could fashion a makeshift bow from bamboo if forced to improvise. This still left the problem of the arrows, although one suggestion is that these would be hidden in the ninja's *amegasa*, possibly disguised as the ribs of the hat. Care would have to be taken, however, for the arrows might well be poison-tipped.

Poison-tipped projectiles might also be fired from their *fukiya*, a blowpipe which could be improvised from a short length of bamboo cane, or even from a simple roll of paper. Darts could be made from cones of paper with needles pushed through to make points. Such devices could also be used to send messages; for instance, to deliver intelligence from inside a castle to besieging forces. The ninja did not need a blowpipe, however, for he could use *fukibari*, or spitting needles, which, with training, could either be spat directly from the mouth or through a very short length of bamboo.

The ninja could also deploy *metsubushi* (eye-closers)— twists or bags of paper, or even hollow eggshells, filled with sand, pepper, and metal shavings. When, flung at an enemy's eyes, these could blind.

FIRE TOOLS

The ninja were experts at using gunpowder for a variety of effects, employing what they called *kaki*, or fire tools. *Kaki* could be used to start and spread fires, as part of classic castle infiltration operations, and to spread panic and confusion in enemy ranks, as well as for direct attack. Types of *kaki* included:

hiya (fire arrows)—gunpowder-filled paper tubes attached to an arrow, which could then be fired at flammable surfaces

hijo (fire sticks)—sticks sharpened to a point at either end and passed through a gunpowder-filled ball of paper, which could be thrown like darts

hidake (fire bamboo)—short lengths of bamboo cane filled with gunpowder to make explosives or to spread fire

hikyu (fire balls)—hollow clay hemispheres, filled with gunpowder and then stuck together to create balls, with projecting fuses so that they could be used as primitive hand grenades, especially if they were also filled with other substances, such as nails or excrement

torinoke (birds' eggs)—blown eggs filled with gunpowder to make explosives or flash/smoke grenades and create an opportunity for the ninja to "vanish"

SPECIALIZED WEAPONS

Some weapons have become specifically associated with ninja. The best-known example is the *shinobi-gama* (secret sickle weapon), a specialized version of the *kusari-gama* (chain and sickle weapon), a length of chain with a sickle-type weapon (i.e., a shaft with a sickle-shaped blade projecting at a right angle) at one end, and a weight on the other. The weighted chain was used to ensnare an opponent's wrist or ankle and drag him off his feet, whereupon the sickle could be used to finish him off. The *shinobi-gama* had a small but extremely sharp blade with a scabbard. These weapons derived from simple agricultural implements available to all farmers, reflecting the ninja's proletarian origins.

KNUCKLE-DUSTERS

Some ninja *ryu* were skilled in the use of special hand gear. *Tekkokagi* or *tekagi* (hand claws) were like knuckle-dusters with claws, spines, or hooks attached. They were slipped over the hand and wrist, and could be worn on the backs of the hands or the palms. They were used for slapping, punching, and parrying (so that a ninja could parry a sword blade with his hands, with the spikes or claws catching the blade so it could be twisted or broken). They also helped with climbing, and could even be worn on the feet like crampons. *Nekkote* or *hokode* (finger claws, or cat's paws) were claws that fit onto the fingers, like extended finger-nails. They might be tipped with poison.

The favorite weapon of the *kunoichi* (female ninja—see page 131) was the *kakute* (horn finger). This was a normal finger ring with a spike or hook, which could be worn on the inside of the palm to hide it from view, but could be used to strike a deadly blow at the unguarded target, especially if tipped with poison. Another ring-weapon was the *shobo*, or *shabo*, a wooden ring with a small project-ing wedge that could be used to target pressure points. This was similar to the *suntetsu*, a small oval piece of wood fixed to the finger with a strap.

Ninja Tools

Because the ninja would actively seek to avoid fighting, equipment other than weapons became important tools. As with weaponry, it was crucial for these tools to be adaptable and serve multiple purposes, so that they could also be used as weapons if necessary. In addition to the fire tools described above, most ninja equipment could be classified into three other categories, defined by function: *noboriki*, or climbing tools; *kaiki*, or opening tools; and *suiki*, or water tools. Many of these items are discussed in the *Bansen Shukai*, an illustrated manual of *ninjutsu* from the seventeenth century.

Climbing Tools

Gaining access to protected structures such as castles, palaces, fortified camps, and houses usually required the ninja to scale walls. Ninja also used trees to gain vantage points, help get over walls, hide from pursuers, or launch ambushes. Climbing skills, therefore, were an important asset to the ninja, who were skilled freestyle climbers, able to use the smallest cracks and handholds to scale high castle walls or gain access to a palace roof at a high speed (see page 93). For maximum climbing ability, however, the right tools were necessary.

LADDERS

Rope was an essential part of basic ninja kit, in the form of the *kaginawa*, or rope-hook. The *tobibashigo* (throwing ladder) was a step-up from the *kaginawa* (a bamboo and rope ladder with iron grappling hooks at one end) and could be used in similar fashion.

The *shinobikagi* (secret hook) was a collapsible bamboo ladder, made by stringing together lengths of bamboo with the rope alternately passing through the middle of a segment and the whole length of another. When the rope was pulled tight, the ladder assembled into alternating vertical and cross-piece elements, creating a stepladder. A grappling hook at one end completed the device.

The *shinobi kumade* (secret rake) was also a collapsible sectioned bamboo device, but when the rope was pulled tight the segments would stack together, forming a rigid pole with a hook at one end. The result was a portable device that could help place a hook or rope over a high wall or branch.

Yet another bamboo-and-rope device was the *shinobitsue* (secret stick)—this was a bamboo staff with a hook at one end and holes along its length. A rope passed through the holes would create loops that could act as footholds, creating a short ladder that could be used for bootstrapping, where the ninja would use it to climb up a short way, grab a handhold to support himself, pull up the *shinobitsue*, and repeat the process. A ladder illustrated in the *Bansen Shukai* appears to be the *shinobi* version of a stepladder: it hinges in the middle so that it folds in two, and has padded ends so that it can be laid soundlessly against a wall.

OTHER CLIMBING TOOLS

Like modern climbers, the ninja used an array of equipment to increase his reach and adhesiveness. The hand-claw devices described above could be used to help climb wooden surfaces. *Ashiko* were spikes for the feet, similar to crampons. *Kasugai* were also similar to crampons, but were hand-held and were used to perform the incredibly tough skill of *gyaku udetate*, a form of upside-down "press-up" in which the ninja would effectively lie, at full length, upside-down on the ceiling. This required extreme upper body and abdominal strength. *Kurorokagi* were ice-axe-like devices that could be used by the ninja to extend his reach, and then once fixed in place could be used for footholds, in the same fashion that a modern climber might use pitons.

OPENING TOOLS

Part of the ninja's job was breaking and entering, which might involve cutting through walls or doors, making gaps in a palisade, or opening a sliding door. A *kunai* was a trowel-like gouging device, with a leaf-shaped blade and saw-tooth edges. It could be used to cut through wood, plaster, and wattle-and-daub—all materials used in the

construction of castle walls in Japan—helping the ninja to quickly dig out an opening. It could also be used as a trowel, for digging out earth, or perhaps for getting under a fence or wall. A *shikoro* was a saw with a triangular blade that could be pressed against the wall and turned one way and then the other, until a hole had been bored that was wide on the ninja's side, but a pinpoint on the far side. This was the perfect configuration for a spy-hole or hole through which to deploy a blowpipe, unnoticed by the occupants of the room. Alternatively, the *shikoro* could be a fold-away version, made of a long, thin blade that hinged along its length to fold up small, or fold into a wooden handle like a penknife.

A *tsubokiri* was a gouging and wedging device, with a handle like that of a corkscrew, attached to a crescent-shaped, two-pronged iron fork. This could be wedged into a narrow gap between timbers and twisted, enlarging the gap wide enough to split the timber or to allow another tool to be used to open the gap still wider.

Once inside a house, castle, or palace, the ninja could use a pair of devices known as *togime* and *shimeki* (jammers and closers) to close sliding doors. These devices were zigzag-shaped iron bars with wedged ends that could be jammed across the slats of a sliding door to prevent them from being opened from the other side. They were useful for trying to delay guards or pursuers, giving the ninja time to carry out his mission or make his getaway.

WATER TOOLS

The ninja had to be able to deal with any terrain or obstacle, including water. Rivers and moats provided a hiding place to the ninja skilled in the use of the *takezutsu* (breathing pipe, similar to a snorkel). Several types of *suiki* (water equipment) are shown in the *Bansen Shukai*, most famously the *mizugumo* (water spiders), devices said to be the speciality of the Koga ninja. Water spiders were a ring of flotation devices (blocks of light wood) tied or chained to a central plank to which the foot was fixed. A ninja could put his weight on the central plank without it sinking due to the floats around it, thus allowing him to walk on water like a waterboatman or spider, or at least to float upright and punt. The *mizugumo* has caused some controversy. At first glance it seems unlikely to work, and indeed modern attempts to replicate and use it have proved unsuccessful. Such considerations give ammunition to modern ninja skeptics (see "Ninja Culture and Controversies," page 152).

A similarly unlikely device is the *ukidaru*, essentially a pair of buckets roped together in which the ninja was supposed to stand, enabling him to punt himself along. More credible is a device composed of a ring of flotation aids (i.e., air-filled sacks), tied together in a fashion similar to the water spider. The ninja could kneel on the central sack while paddling himself along, with the surrounding sacks providing buoyancy and stability. The *shinobibune* (secret boat) was a prefabricated, collapsible, lightweight frame that could be easily carried and concealed, as well as rapidly assembled. It could be covered with waterproofed cloth to create a makeshift boat, or attached to flotation aids to make a raft. Aids said to have been used by the ninja included half-filled jars of water and turtle shells.

The simplest flotation device a ninja could use was an item of clothing, such as his trousers, tied off to create a bag and then filled with air. If the ninja had to swim, he could make use of *mizukakigeta* (water sandals), which were essentially sandals with paddles attached to create a primitive form of flipper, like those used by modern frogmen.

ADDITIONAL KIT

A ninja might have carried an array of miscellaneous items that don't fit into the categories described above. The ninja was expected to have detailed knowledge of herbal and medicinal lore for medical and survival purposes, as well as the all-important task of preparing and administering poisons.

FOOD

Besides herbs and a supply of rice, the ninja also packed specialized foods designed to maintain energy levels while on operations. According to a modern recipe, one type of tablet was made from honey, grains (such as wheat), carrots, rice, and sake. The *Bansen Shukai* gives a similar

recipe for what it calls "hunger pills," which includes ginseng, rice, flour, and potato, soaked in sake for three years and then formed into little balls. There is also a recipe for thirst pills (consisting of pickled plums), intended to help ninja stave off dehydration while on "stakeout" in an enemy house or castle. Sesame seeds or leeks were also chewed or sucked to stimulate saliva production to help stave off thirst.

SOUND AND LIGHT

The *saoto hikigane* was a type of ear trumpet made from a metal cone or tapered cylinder and worked along the same principle as putting a glass against a wall to amplify sounds coming from the other side. This was useful for spying and locating guards.

Another piece of kit was the *gando* (eyelight), a type of specialized lantern. It consisted of a candle mounted on gimbals inside a cup or bell-shaped cover that allowed the ninja to direct light in one direction only, to avoid giving away his presence unnecessarily. The gimbals allowed the candle to remain upright and lit regardless of the direction in which the lantern was pointed.

忍者

Fall down
seven times,
stand up
eight.

—*Japanese Proverb*

up in a manner that emphasized the fundamental psychological skills and personal values he would need. For instance, the infant ninja trainee had an upbringing that emphasized awareness of the world around him, which laid the foundations for highly developed awareness in adult life—an important virtue for one whose life and livelihood depends on stealth and espionage.

Chapter 3
Ninjutsu— Principles and Training

Ninjutsu, the art of stealth, refers to the specific physical skills learned and practiced by the ninja, most notably martial arts. It also refers to a wider range of disciplines, including practical, intellectual, psychological, and spiritual training, as well as a more holistic concept—that of a world-view, or a way of looking at the world and existing in it accordingly.

Today, *ninjutsu* training mainly involves learning martial arts in one of the several schools, or *ryu*, maintained around the world. However, for the historical ninja, as interpreted by contemporary writers, *ninjutsu* training was a lifelong process of total immersion that began in early infancy. In other words, it was an upbringing rather than simply a training program, informed by the fact that, as Jay Sensei puts it, "historically, *ninjutsu* was a profession inherited at birth."

A NINJA UPBRINGING

Scholars differ on the exact pattern that *ninjutsu* training followed, but all agree on the broad outlines. Training began at birth, and the future ninja was brought up in a manner that emphasized the fundamental psychological skills and personal values he would need. For instance, the infant ninja-trainee had an upbringing that emphasized awareness of the world around him, which laid the foundations for highly developed awareness in adult life—an important virtue for one whose life and livelihood depended on stealth and espionage. From an early age, play became an extended training exercise, with games and leisure time shaped to enhance physical qualities, such as balance and agility, and mental qualities, such as adaptability and resourcefulness.

According to Stephen Hayes, body-conditioning started at age nine, with basic unarmed combat (i.e., punching and kicking). Introductory sword skills were taught at ages ten to twelve. Specialized weapons and tools were introduced in the early teens, and by the late teens the more advanced and cerebral elements of *ninjutsu* were taught, with the young trainee learning about acting, practical psychology, herbs and medicines, espionage, tactics and strategy, and, eventually, a host of other disciplines, from meteorology to architecture.

Jay Sensei describes a similar system, but with a more formal categorization. At first the ninja child was educated in the ways of nature and how to live in harmony with it. Formal training began at age eight, with *shinren* (heart training), which involved the training of the senses and reflexes. This included skills and disciplines such as being observant and aware, remaining calm under pressure, being able to withstand extremes and endure hardships, and being able to respond instinctively to challenges and adapt to changing circumstances.

Next came *tairen* (body training), which involved body-conditioning and exercise to boost strength, endurance, and agility. This was followed by the most advanced stage, *chiren* (knowledge training), which covered everything from strategy, meteorology, medicine, explosives, and farming, to signaling, music and dancing, psychology, disguise, and acting.

MODERN NINJUTSU

Masaaki Hatsumi, a renowned modern *ninjutsu* master, says that there are eight core disciplines in modern *ninjutsu*, known as the Eight Methods, or the *Happo Hiken*.

They are:

1. Body skills and rope throwing
2. Unarmed fighting
3. Spear and halberd (a very long-shafted ax) arts
4. Staff and stick arts
5. Throwing blades
6. Use of fire and water
7. Military fortification, strategy, and tactics
8. Concealment

He also mentions "the secret sword arts" as a potential ninth method.

Other sources talk about the *Ninja Juhakkei*, or the Eighteen Ninja Skills, which relate to the *Bugei Juhappan* (the Eighteen Samurai Fighting Arts). These eighteen disciplines are:

1. Seishin-teki kyōyō (spiritual refinement)
2. Taijutsu (unarmed combat)
3. Ninja ken (sword fighting)
4. Bōjutsu (stick and staff fighting)
5. Shurikenjutsu (throwing blades)
6. Sōjutsu (spear fighting)

7. Naginatajutsu (naginata fighting)

8. Kusarigamajutsu (chain and sickle weapon)

9. Kayakujutsu (fire and explosives)

10. Hensōjutsu (disguise and impersonation)

11. Shinobi-iri (stealth and entering methods)

12. Bajutsu (horsemanship)

13. Sui-ren (water training)

14. Bōryaku (military strategy)

15. Chōhō (espionage and spying)

16. Intonjutsu (escaping and concealment)

17. Tenmon (meteorology)

18. Chi-mon (geography)

BASIC PHYSICAL TRAINING

The ninja was expected to demonstrate almost superhuman physical prowess. He had to be able to cover great distances on foot; cope with all types of terrain; survive extremes of temperature, hunger, and thirst; move swiftly and silently; cross rivers and moats; climb high walls; cling to ceilings; remain immobile for hours, even days; defeat better-armed and better-armored enemies, even when heavily outnumbered; and then escape. Accordingly, physical conditioning to boost endurance, strength, and agility was an important element of ninja training.

FISTS OF FURY

The ninja had to practice a variety of exacting exercises. *Te, ude,* and *kata* (hand, wrist, and arm training, respectively) were intended to strengthen the fist, the grip, and the arms, and also to harden the hands and fingers so that they could withstand extreme force and be used as weapons or tools. In particular, the young ninja trained for hours with punching exercises, kneeling on the ground to punch holes filled with sand. Later, as his fists got stronger, the holes were filled with gravel, pebbles, stones, rocks, and pieces of metal, in succession. He also trained by hitting trees.

GRIPPING

Specific gripping training, known as *akuryoku*, helped to strengthen the hands, wrists, arms, and shoulders, and to harden the fingers and hands. Exercises included repeatedly clenching the fist against the resistance of water and sand. The *sunamochi* exercise involved holding clay pots filled with sand at arm's length for hours on end. *Takeippon* was a tough and painful drill in which the trainee attempted to pull or tear one stalk of bamboo from a tightly bound bundle. This put tremendous strain on the fingertips and nails. *Kakejin* ("the hanging man") was another challenging exercise where the trainee hung from a branch while wearing sacks of stones around his shoulders and/or on his belt, for up to eight hours. This kind of endurance was necessary for ninja tasks such as hanging from the rafters of a room while lying in wait for a target.

DIET

An important part of basic training was diet. The ninja had their roots among the simple farming folk, and their traditional diet reflected this. According to Masaaki Hatsumi, the basic ninja diet "consists of brown rice, tofu, sesame, miso soup, no salt, no sugar, uncooked food, and colored vegetables." Hatsumi also points out that while unpolished brown rice would be the day-to-day staple,

when on operations, the ninja might switch to white rice, which had a more accessible energy content. In terms of general approach to eating and mealtimes, a ninja was never supposed to grow reliant on a routine, but always be willing to adapt to whatever was offered.

RUNNING AND JUMPING

These fairly basic physical disciplines were all-important to the ninja, who practiced a range of exercises to improve speed, endurance, and agility. Basic *ashi*, or running exercises, included sprinting with a straw hat placed against the chest. The hat was not secured in any way, and had to be kept in place by the pressure of the air as the ninja ran, requiring him to maintain a minimum speed. For the "thirty-foot cloth" exercise, the ninja would run with a long swath of cloth attached to him, which would trail behind him to act as a wind-brake and increase air resistance. Running with sacks of rocks was another drill.

The cumulative purpose of all these drills was to train the ninja to perform amazing feats of long-distance running. According to Jay Sensei, a ninja "could run between 100-120 km/day [62-75 miles/day] at a speed of just under 20 km/h [12 mph]. A modern marathon runner runs about 50 km [31 miles] at 20 km/h [12 mph] whereas the ninja, carrying all his weapons and climbing equipment, could run twice the distance [at the same speed]." This allowed a ninja to move quickly between his home base and the theater of operations where he was employed, without needing a horse—the prerogative of the samurai. The ninja was self-reliant and could move at his own pace; he could handle any terrain or climate without serious reduction of mobility.

WALK LIKE A NINJA

The ninja had to be able to move with total control, and, if necessary, at high speed, in any situation. Accordingly, he was trained in a number of special walking techniques. *Ko ashi*, or walking with small, stabbing steps, like a crane, allowed the ninja to move through leaf litter or shallow water with a minimum of noise and disturbance. *Yoko aruki*, or sideways walking, allowed fluid movement through narrow corridors or staying tight to a wall to avoid detection. The ninja was expected to master this style to a point where he could run in this fashion at a high speed. For *nuki ashi*, a sweeping step, the ninja transferred weight gently from one foot to the next, minimizing the peaks of pressure produced by normal walking. This helped him to walk silently, especially on creaky floorboards that might reveal his approach. A common exercise for perfecting quiet walking was to cover the floor with sheets of paper and practice walking silently across them. *Henso hoko jutsu*, known as "the entertainer's walk," is a sort of drunken stagger that the ninja used as a disguise.

Heikou (equilibrium) is the name given to balance training, such as bamboo walking. This is basically tightrope
walking, but along a bamboo cane placed between two
supports, rather than along a rope. Ninja would use *geta*,
wooden sandals with slats projecting like mini-stilts, and
perfect their balance by learning to walk across rough terrain in them.

JUMPING

Among the attributes that came to be associated with the
ninja (see page 107) the most magical was the ability to fly.
Perhaps this had its basis in their jumping and acrobatic
skills, which they developed to help them get over high
walls at high speed. Jumping training in general was called
tobu, and included the ability to leap far and high in any
direction from any position or stance. Specialized skills
included the *futari jinba* (two-man horse) for launching a
ninja onto or over a wall. One ninja would crouch at the
base of the wall with his back to it, while the other would
run up and use the first one's cupped hands as a launching
point. At the same time, the first ninja would straighten
his legs with maximum force, adding his momentum to
the jumper's leap. In the *sannin jinba* (three-man horse), a
similar procedure was followed, but with one ninja standing with his back to the wall, one crouched in front of
him, and the third running up and getting a simultane-
ous leg and armpit boost from the other two. Alternative

versions included one ninja balancing on the hands of another, who would run at the wall and launch his companion at the last moment; or a number of ninja forming a sort of human pyramid, up which a companion could run. The ninja also trained in using spears, pikes, or halberds as pole vaults for crossing moats or high walls.

HIDING AND ESCAPING

Ideally, the ninja would never have to fight because he would go undetected; therefore, hiding and escaping were central elements of *ninjutsu*. Ninja were trained in *mudo* (stillness), which involved learning to lie in wait, possibly in cramped, awkward, cold, hot, wet, or otherwise uncomfortable conditions, for hours or even days on end. They had to be able to do this in absolute silence, without cramping or tiring, so that when the moment came they could swing into action with their full capabilities. As part of this training, ninja learned to control their breathing and slow their heartbeat and metabolism to a minimum to limit their need for food and water. One simple trick they used was to block one nostril with cotton to reduce the volume of respiration while they were hiding.

OUT OF SIGHT

Another of the magical qualities ascribed to the ninja is invisibility. This may have derived from their uncanny powers of hiding, linked to their use of *ongyo*, or hiding forms. They were trained to hide behind rocks, in reeds, on roofs, in the eaves and rafters, up trees, and even underwater (using the *takezutsu*, or snorkel). The ninja was an expert in lowering his profile by blending in with his cover, minimizing exposed and reflective surfaces, using shade, and maintaining stillness.

TYING AND ESCAPING BONDS

The ninja had to perfect the fine art of *musubi*—the art of knots and tying people up. This included escape techniques for getting free of bonds if captured. He learned to dislocate joints and contort his body, which was also useful for fitting into tiny spaces or containers for hiding himself. Together with many complex knotting schemes, the ninja would master the simple cross-thumb technique, ideal for incapacitating a rival ninja. The prisoner's thumbs would be tied behind his back in a criss-cross fashion, preventing movement in any direction. The bound thumbs would then be tied to his big toes.

SURVIVAL SKILLS

Ninja typically worked alone or in small groups, and could not rely on support or supply lines. This meant that during an operation, and while traveling to and from one, the ninja had to be able to fend for himself, living off the land and using his woodcraft and survival skills to stay fed, sheltered, and healthy.

One of the most basic tricks the ninja learned was how to cook rice without utensils by wrapping a handful of rice in a cloth, soaking it in water, and burying it under a campfire. The *Bansen Shukai* advises that seawater can be made drinkable by boiling it in unglazed earthenware, which

will supposedly absorb the salt. Alternatively, the ninja was trained in a number of ways of finding drinking water in the wild. One method involved planting a feather in the ground near a suspected source and returning later to see whether it had collected dew, which indicated whether there was indeed moisture around. Others included looking for anthills (ants favored spots near water sources), recognizing water-loving plants, and even putting an ear to the ground to listen for nearby water-courses.

Knowledge of plants and other natural resources was an important feature of ninja education. A ninja knew which plants, berries, and fungi were edible, and which could be used to make medicines and poisons. While en route to an operation, he might collect the poisons he needed for his weapons. Possible sources of poisons included aconitum (wolfsbane), datura (Jimson weed), and fugu (pufferfish).

ORIENTEERING

Ninja were skilled cross-country navigators. They could navigate by the stars or find their way using a *jishaku* (magnet), which was a small piece of lodestone (magnetic iron ore) placed on a leaf and floated on water (e.g., in a puddle or cupped in the hand). Thus able to rotate, the lodestone would align itself with the Earth's magnetic field, acting as a primitive compass. To calculate how much distance they had covered, ninja counted (or accurately estimated) the number of strides they had made and multiplied this by the known length of a stride. Alternatively, they might have a finely calibrated knowledge of their speed when moving over different terrains and inclines, and use this to calculate their progress.

The third element needed for accurate navigation, after direction and distance, is timing. Ninja were expert at using natural clocks, such as the shadows cast by objects. The *Bansen Shukai* outlines an amusing though farfetched method, known as *nekome* (cat's eyes), where it was possible to tell the time by observing the dilation of a cat's pupils—wider for earlier or later times, narrower the closer to noon it is.

ACTING AND THE ART OF DISGUISE

Like any good spy, the ninja was a master of the art of disguise. Disguise allowed him to travel incognito, and helped with infiltration operations. One ninja handbook, *The Ninja and Their Secret Fighting Art,* lists the *shichiho de* (seven disguises):

1. **Yamabushi:** mountain warrior-priests who were historically associated with the ninja and shared many attributes (e.g., outsider and outlaw status, lurking in the mountains, spiritual and martial arts training)
2. **Sarugaku:** dancers and entertainers
3. **Komuso:** mendicant, flute-playing monks, notable for their huge straw hats that covered the entire head
4. **Shukke:** Buddhist priests and monks, some sects of which traditionally carried a large flute, called the *shakuhaci,* which a ninja could employ as a club
5. **Akindo:** merchants and traders
6. **Ronin:** masterless samurai for hire
7. **Gakushi:** musician or strolling player

Note that all of these professions are itinerant; someone traveling in such a guise would not arouse suspicion, and would be able to go where he pleased, relatively unmolested. Other guises the ninja might adopt included doctor, tramp or beggar, farmer, soldier, or fisherman.

METHOD ACTING

Disguise for the ninja was not simply a matter of dressing up in a costume. The ninja learned to become totally immersed in the role that he was adopting, mastering the psychological, physical, and technical aspects with total commitment. For instance, if adopting the guise of a musician, the ninja was expected to be proficient in the instrument he carried; if adopting the guise of a holy man, he had to be fully conversant with the philosophy, rites, and rituals involved. He was expected to learn the exact dialect of the role he was adopting, as well as the language and jargon. Ninja posing as disfigured beggars might use poisons to actually disfigure themselves; a trick for pretending to be blind was to wear fish scales in the eyes to mimic cataracts. The point was not to act at the profession or role, but actually to become it. The highest goal was to achieve what has been described as "artless naturalness."

NINJA PSYCHOLOGY

The ninja did not rely on force of arms alone to achieve his mission. He was expected to be a master psychologist as well as a swordsman. Ninja psychology was both intrapersonal (i.e., involving his own psyche) and interpersonal (i.e., involving other people).

PERSONAL PSYCHOLOGY

The tenets of ninja psychology are adaptability and endurance. Indeed, the latter is suggested by one of the meanings of the kanji character *nin*: forbearance, the quality of patient endurance. It could be interpreted thus: The ninja's goal is fixed, while his method is not. He is expected to use any means necessary and endure any hardship to achieve his end. He is mindful at all times of his environment, and attuned to natural and manmade occurrences and processes. He is not inflexible or rigid in his thinking, and is, therefore, able to adjust his plans to take into account new developments, restrictions, or opportunities. His response to people, events, or situations is dictated by them, not according to predetermined mindsets. Accordingly the ninja is good at seeing what is, not simply what he assumes or wants.

Traditionally, there were also darker aspects of ninja psychology. Unlike the samurai, ninja did not place a pre-

mium on honor. A ninja was not above using underhanded or amoral means to achieve his ends, including betrayal and murder. Just as he placed little value on the lives of others, a ninja had to be prepared to accept his own death. Sometimes his mission required him to be captured and tortured (see page 126).

PSYCHOLOGICAL WARFARE

Ninjutsu training emphasized the psychological aspects of combat and warfare, particularly since it was probably derived in part from the writings of Sun Tzu (see page 126), the ancient Chinese theorist of war who emphasized the role of psychology in conflict. Ninja were sometimes specifically used by generals to carry out special missions to humiliate or demoralize the enemy, such as capturing their standards or assassinating their top men. For instance, in the chronicle *Ou Eikyo Gunki*, it is related that during the siege of Hataya Castle, a valiant ninja, under cover of night, stole an enemy commander's personal standard from a guard and planted it on the castle ramparts. It goes on to say, "When dawn broke, men from the attacking force saw it and said: 'This is mortifying. Not only has this tiny castle not fallen, but we have been so negligent that a flag has been stolen.' "

Sometimes ninja units used guerrilla tactics to wear down opponents and keep them in a state of perpetual tension, exhausting them and breaking down their mental defenses.

An example is given by the chronicle *Iran-ki*, which tells how the Iga ninja who were cornered in a castle by the army of Oda Nobuo (son of Oda Nobunaga) harried their foes. The ninja reduced the besieging troops to a state of nervous exhaustion by constant nighttime raids. No matter how carefully the besieger's camp was defended, each night more guards were picked off by the ninja: "Over a hundred men were killed, and because of this the enemy were placed in fear and trembling. Their alertness decreased because they could not rest at all."

FEAR FACTOR

Over time, the ninja could use their fearsome reputation to their advantage. The ninja's mystique and aura allowed him to enter combat with a distinct edge over his opponent. Fear of ninja infiltration might make guards jittery and nervous, which led to mistakes and opportunities for the ninja. In particular, it made it easier for the ninja to sow discord, panic, and confusion, a major part of their operating mode (see page 129).

MAGIC AND MYSTIQUE

Part of the fear that ninja inspired derived from the myths and legends that arose around them. In folklore and popular tales, ninja possessed super powers such as invisibility and the power of flight (see page 175). Possibly these were linked to ninja prowess at hiding and escaping, and jumping and climbing, respectively. They may also reflect the cultural origins of the ninja in tales of the *tengu*, which are fierce bird-man demons that played a role in Japanese folklore similar to elves and goblins in the West.

Another source could be the association between ninja and *yamabushi*. These warrior-monks (who were also linked in folklore to the *tengu*) were famed for their mountain-pilgrimages, during which it was said they could attain magical powers, such as conversing with animals, curing illness, and controlling flames. A favored destination for such pilgrimages was the mountainous Iga-Koga region (the ninja heartland), and a favorite disguise of the ninja was as *yamabushi*—so it may have been natural for the two groups to become conflated to some extent. In some ninja histories, En no Gyoja, the founder of Shugendo— the Buddhist sect to which *yamabushi* subscribed—is also said to have been the first ninja.

Even today some *ninjutsu* practitioners make claims about quasi-mystical abilities, such as the ability to focus and project *chi* (bio-energy), so that they can exert force with

little or no contact. The Togakure-*ryu* even teaches that a ninja can develop the psychic ability to perceive *sakki*—the force of the killer—a kind of psychic emanation of malice from an enemy towards the ninja. Once able to detect this *sakki*, a ninja can be forewarned with precise premonitions of danger that allow him to avoid not only blows from an enemy in the vicinity, but even bullets, arrows, and bombs launched from a distance or remotely detonated. This "sixth sense" is said to be possible because a spiritually evolved ninja can tune into a higher level of consciousness. Whether or not such incredible claims are possible, it is clear that even today *ninjutsu* practitioners continue to surround their discipline with layers of mysticism.

MAKING THE SIGNS

Tales of ninja magicians may also owe something to the practice of *in-o-musubi* (making the signs). This involved performing *kettsuin* or *kuju-in*, which are ritual-magical finger movements and combinations, where the fingers are curled and interlaced in various patterns, supposedly to channel mystical *chi* energy and produce magical effects and cast spells. Historian Stephen Turnbull traces the finger signs back to Buddhist *mudra* (hand gestures), often seen in statues of the Buddha, which were brought to Japan in the seventh century A.D. by the monk Kobo Daishi, founder of the Shingon sect.

The ninja utilized finger signs for numbers one through nine, and these could be elaborated into a system of

eighty-one signs (nine was a magical number). For instance, performing the correct *kettsuin* before going into
action was said to confer the power of invisibility. Other legends claim the finger signs could hypnotize enemies. Whether or not the ninja really believed they were imbued with
these powers is not clear—perhaps these rituals and signs
were simply a form of preparatory meditation, and the tales
of their effects are simply metaphors for the way in which a
ninja would attain the correct state of mind.

Also associated with the Shingon sect was the use of magical charms and talismans. These included spells written on
paper in blood, which were said to inspire courage or even
to wound enemies.

UNARMED COMBAT

The ninja were famous for their mastery of the martial arts, and today most *ninjutsu* training focuses on this aspect almost exclusively. The various weapons techniques are complex and hard to describe without direct instruction. However, it is possible to give a useful overview of the unarmed combat techniques, including the postures and the hand and fist configurations. (*N.B.:* These descriptions are not intended to be used for instruction, and readers should never attempt to replicate any of the moves or actions described below.)

NINJA FIGHTING STYLE

To some extent, the *ninjutsu* approach to unarmed combat reflects the overall philosophy of *ninjutsu* as a whole. The ninja does not follow rigid rules or strictly circumscribed techniques. He is adaptable and flexible. He does not restrict himself to a set repertoire of moves, nor does he follow a strict choreography to generate his fighting style. His technique is dictated by circumstance, the environment, and, of course, the opponent. Many ninja moves and stances have been developed to adapt to and neutralize the opponent's moves, to avoid playing to his strengths, or even to turn his strengths into weaknesses. For instance, an important principle in *ninjutsu* is *ma ai* (distancing), where the ninja uses close-in moves (such as grappling and throwing) against a fighter who specializes in distance

moves (such as kicks), or distance moves against a fighter who is skilled at close fighting.

The emphasis is on results over style, on practical, effective moves with an economy of movement, often derived from the practical, lethal intent of the original system. In other words, ninja technique was designed and developed for the purposes of real fighting, not for sport or exercise. Some of the particularly specialized techniques, such as the Togakure-*ryu's* art of using *tekage* (hand claws) to fight an opponent armed with a sword, reflect the ninja heritage as low-social-status, anti-samurai outsiders, making do with whatever came to hand.

Unarmed combat *ninjutsu* breaks down into two main approaches: *daken taijutsu* and *ju taijutsu*. *Daken taijutsu* is the art of attacking the bones, and involves strikes, kicks, and blocks. *Ju taijutsu*, described as "the relaxed body method," involves grappling and throwing. Although these divisions make it sound as though the former is equivalent to karate and the latter to judo, *ninjutsu* masters insist that this is a superficial reading, and that in fact *ninjutsu* encompasses and supersedes such categorizations and pigeon-holes.

NINJA FISTS

Central to *daken taijutsu* are the hand positions, or fists, used in the various moves. Different positions have different functions or roles, and are applicable when striking different parts of the body.

Shikan ken (extended knuckle fist): This is formed by bending the first and second finger joints but not the knuckles, with the thumb folded along the side of the first finger, to give a long, sharp, shallow fist where all the force is concentrated through the sharp leading edge. It is best used for striking bone, especially facial bones, breastbones, and the sides of the middle ribs, in order to inflict pain or break the bone.

Fudo ken (clenched fist): This is the conventional fist shape, with the fingers bent at the knuckles to give a broad, flat impact area. It is used for strikes against the edges of bones, particularly the nose, the jaw, the lower edges of the ribs, and the bones of the arms and legs.

Boshi ken (thumb-drive fist): The Boshi ken position involves curling the knuckles and joints so that the second joint of the first finger projects ahead of the others, and is reinforced by pressing the thumb into the hollow of the second joint. The aim is to give a hard point through which force can be focused; this is used to make precision strikes on nerve centers and places where muscle is stretched thin over

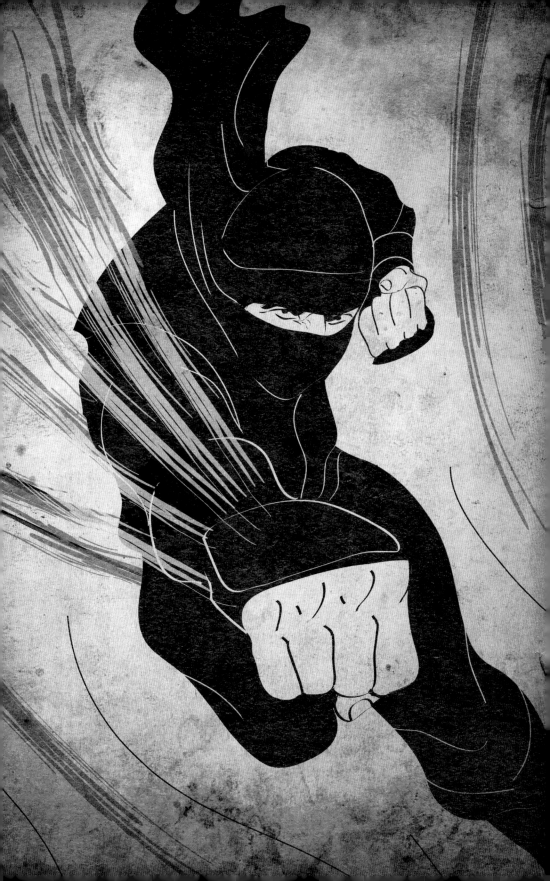

bone. Target areas include the sides of the neck, the sides of the upper ribs, and the solar plexus.

Shuto (sword hand): This is an open hand. It is a configuration, similar to a classic "karate chop" hand, made by holding the hand flat and bending the fingers at the knuckle so that the planes of the palm and the fingers are at a forty-five degree angle to one another. It is used to stun an opponent or for bone-breaking strikes, especially against the limbs, joints, and neck.

NINJA STANCE

A central element of the *ninjutsu* approach to unarmed combat is the *kamae* (body posture or stance). Stephen Hayes calls this "the physical embodiment of mental attitude," and it dictates how the ninja responds to his opponent's moves and what moves of his own he can launch. It is here that one of the primary differences between *ninjutsu* and other martial arts systems becomes apparent, because in *ninjutsu* there is no fixed stance and no set rules about posture. The ninja moves fluidly between whichever stances are called for given the situation and the opponent. There are four main types of stance, each of which is said to have an association or affinity with one of the four elements (a scheme that applies to many aspects of *ninjutsu*).

Shizen no kamae (natural posture): This posture is associated with the element earth, and to the untrained eye looks nothing like a combat posture. The ninja simply stands upright, facing his opponent, his feet slightly apart, and his arms hanging by his side. This is the ninja's default posture; it allows him to segue into any move or sequence of moves, as the occasion demands.

Ichimonji no kamae (defensive posture): This posture is associated with the element water, and is used when on the defensive. The ninja turns sideways to his opponent and squats slightly, with his knees bent and his feet spread wide. His front foot points forward, while his back one is at right angles to it. His right arm is bent so that his elbow guards the ribs, while his left is extended in front. This position keeps his center of gravity low, and by leading with his hips he can swivel quickly to block the opponent while still generating extreme force.

Jumonji no kamae (offensive posture): This posture is associated with the element fire, and is used to launch attacking moves. The ninja stands up mostly straight, with slightly flexed knees and the feet planted slightly further apart than his hips. He has one foot leading a little but with the toes slightly pointing in, so that the body is turned at a very slight angle to the opponent. He holds his fists just in front of his chin, crossed at the wrist, with his elbows covering his ribs.

Hira no kamae (receiving posture): This posture is associated with the element air or wind. Despite its open appearance, it is partly a defensive posture, good for blocking kicks and punches and then segueing into attack. The ninja stands facing his opponent with his feet spread slightly and his knees flexed a bit. His arms are spread wide and raised above the shoulders, with the palms facing forward. He can swivel quickly at the waist, which allows him to block punches or kicks before they can land.

To make these positions work the ninja needs lightning reflexes and a well-conditioned body, but the majority of the force he can apply comes from good technique. By moving in the correct manner and shifting his center of gravity properly, the ninja can channel all his kinetic energy into each move, or cancel out an opponent's energy.

忍 者

All warfare
is based on
deception.
There is
no place where
espionage is
not used.

—*Sun Tzu*

who the shôgun and the classes there were the ones
actually in charge of operations. They would negotiate with
daimyo wishing to hire ninja, and would then plan and run
the operations. Most of the best-known ninja in history
were chunin. Carrying out the operations were the genin,
the foot soldiers and ground agents. Genin were expected
to follow orders without question, and be willing to sacri-
ce their lives for the mission and/or the clan.

Chapter 4
Ninjutsu—Operations

Ninjutsu evolved as a means to an end—a system of thought and practice that enabled its practitioners to serve as highly effective covert operations agents, able to carry out a range of functions including scouting, reconnaissance, espionage, castle infiltration, and assassination.

THE NINJA HIERARCHY

In the Iga and Koga provinces, the ninja were organized into clans or families, much like the mainstream samurai. The ninja, however, had a specific hierarchal organization, which helped them to maintain security and secrecy in a fashion similar to modern intelligence or underground forces. At the top of the hierarchy, heading each clan, was the *shonin* (also known as *jonin*). Some of these *shonin* were humble farmers, others were more like small-scale *daimyo*. Some were referred to as samurai in the chronicles. The *shonin* was a respected and revered family figurehead, who might not have played much part in planning or running operations, although a notable example of a *shonin* who did get his hands dirty was Hattori "Devil" Hanzo, who campaigned with and guarded Tokugawa Ieyasu (see page 157).

After the *shonin* came the *chunin*. These were the men actually in charge of operations. They would negotiate with *daimyo* wishing to hire ninja, and would then plan and run the operations. Most of the best-known ninja in history were *chunin*. Carrying out the operations were the *genin*, the foot soldiers and ground agents. *Genin* were expected to follow orders without question, and be willing to sacrifice their lives for the mission and/or the clan. *Chunin* and their *genin* operated in a cell system where *genin* did not necessarily know other genin and dealt with only one *chunin*, unaware of who the others were. This helped preserve the security of the system if a *genin* was captured and tortured.

SETTING OUT

Once tasked with a mission, the *genin* entered the first phase of the operation, called *tabidatsu* (setting out). He might travel cross-country, keeping off the roads and away from people, making full use of his training in distance-running, navigation, orienteering, survival, and woodcraft. With these skills, he could travel light and fast, evading detection by enemy forces or spies. Alternatively, he might use his skills of disguise and acting to travel by more conventional routes, allowing him to enter towns and villages without arousing suspicion. These skills were part of the *yonin* (sunlight secret) branch of ninjutsu, where work was done in the open. These contrasted with the *innin* (shadow secrets) used for more covert work, such as espionage and infiltration. For these operations the motto was, according to Stephen Hayes, "Make the night your friend and the darkness your cloak of invisibility."

ESPIONAGE

The Japanese learned from Sun Tzu that espionage was a
key component of successful warfare, and the evolution of
the ninja was partly a response to this development. Accordingly, espionage became a major part of *ninjutsu*, and
trainee ninja were instructed in its principles and techniques. In the system of espionage that ninja were taught
(which derived from Sun Tzu), there were six main stages.

AGENTS

Stage one involved planting or recruiting agents. The five
methods for doing this could be classified using the system
of elements, where each method was associated with one
of the four elements (earth, water, fire, and wind) or the
fifth fundamental force (the void, or the absence of any
of the four elements). Elemental schemes were useful as
mnemonics, but also related to the underlying philosophi-
cal and spiritual tenets of *ninjutsu*.

The earth approach involved sending an agent to a likely
target region before open hostilities were declared, so that
he would have time to embed himself, develop networks of
informants, discover the best vantage points for reconnaissance, etc. The water approach involved allowing an agent
to be captured so that he could feed false information
to his captors. In one form of this ruse, known as *keika*
(firefly), a ninja who was captured (not necessarily inten-
tionally) would, under interrogation, feed his captors false

information. The captors would naturally be suspicious of the information, but a second ninja would deliberately allow himself to be captured and provide the same false information, thus convincing the mistrustful enemy. An alternative form of the water approach was to use *kunoichi* (female ninja) in a "honey-trap" operation (see page 131).

The fire approach involved developing someone from the target region or from enemy ranks as an agent, by turning them through bribery, blackmail, flattery, or deceit. Well-placed civilians or actual members of enemy forces might be targets. Enemy personnel could also be used against their erstwhile employers as conduits for feeding them false information. For the wind approach, the ninja identified enemy agents in their own camp, and either let them think they remained undetected while feeding them false information or turned them so that they became double agents. The void method involved planting agents for long periods—possibly decades—ahead of when they would be needed, as "sleepers." These sleepers might obtain access to information or people in positions of trust, such as servants or maids, personal retainers, officials, stewards, etc. When needed, they could start collecting intelligence, spreading disinformation, or "spiking" the enemy's intelligence network (by identifying and/or eliminating their agents). This approach was also known as *netane* (the sleeping seed), and could involve agents seeded in their teenage years.

FROM STRATEGY TO TACTICS

Once agents were in place and streams of intelligence were established, subsequent stages progressed down a hierarchy of intelligence information, from the highest, most general intelligence to the most specific on-the-ground intelligence. Stage two entailed determining the enemy's goals. This meant learning the enemy's overall intentions and war aims (his long-term strategic goals). Stage three involved determining the enemy's strategy, or discovering how the enemy intended to achieve his goals. This encompassed discerning the enemy's strategic plans and their details, including overall force characteristics (such as how many and what types of troops), logistics and supply chains, dates of major troop movements and planned offensives, identities of key personnel, codes and signals that would be used, and details of the enemy's intelligence networks.

Stage four called for sowing confusion, which meant attempting to interfere with the enemy's plans, tricking him into making incorrect plans, and creating dissension and distrust within his ranks—in particular, distrust of the intelligence his own espionage operation was feeding him. This could be achieved by using planted and double agents to feed the enemy false or misleading information. Stage five involved determining the enemy's tactics, which meant learning the details of enemy troop placement and movement, the number and nature of the units involved and their battlefield disposition, and plans of attack and defense. The was the counterespionage stage, where the

ninja's intention was to preserve the security of his own goals, strategy, and tactics, and to discover what the enemy knew or thought he knew about them.

KUNOICHI

Kunoichi, or female ninja, hardly feature in the historical record, but this may simply be because their work was even less visible than that of their male counterparts. *Kunoichi* had to undergo rigorous training similar to that for male ninja. They were much less likely to be used as commando-style warriors, and much more likely to infiltrate the enemy's domestic set-up as spies or assassins. In particular, a *kunoichi* was expected to sacrifice her virtue for the ninja cause if necessary, and might be used in a classic intelligence operation known as the "honey-trap." This entailed a female agent using her wiles to lure an enemy target into the bedroom, where he could be compromised in a number of ways: his sexual indiscretion could be used to blackmail him; he could be drugged and/or robbed; or he could be coaxed to let important information slip through pillow talk. Female ninja posing as servants or maids might be allowed a high level of access to the most secure parts of a *daimyo's* palace or mansion; thanks to their lowly status, they could escape notice as they eavesdropped. *Kunoichi* posing as courtesans would gain even more intimate access to high-ranking targets, and by using weapons such as the *kakute* (horn finger; see page 67), could act as deadly assassins even when naked.

SIGNALS

An important part of any intelligence work is communicating information back to headquarters in a manner that will not be detected. To do this, ninja used a variety of codes and media. They might have left color-coded rice scattered at a campsite or other location, which would not attract too much notice but could be interpreted by other ninja. This technique, known as *irogome*, featured rice grains colored red, black, white, yellow, and blue. Combinations could be used to pass on simple messages, such as "all clear" or "enemy patrol in area."

If ninja were traveling in disguise as musicians, entertainers, or singing priests, they could use their music to pass on information by playing of special, coded songs. The *seki hitsu* (stone pen; see page 55) could be used to leave messages, possibly employing a code like the one described in the *Bansen Shukai*, where complex Chinese ideograms were used in place of more conventional Japanese characters (this is technically known as a substitution cipher). The *Bansen Shukai* also describes an outlandish method of battlefield signaling that could be used to ensure secure communications between a mounted ninja on reconnaissance and his commander back in camp: the ninja would walk the horse in certain patterns, which could be interpreted by an informed observer but would be meaningless to the enemy.

CASTLE INFILTRATION

One of the key roles of the ninja during their glory years
of the fifteenth and sixteenth centuries was the infiltration
and storming of castles. Ninja had the unique skills to be
able to cross moats, scale walls, cut through palisades, and
climb over parapets, all without detection. Once inside
they could gain valuable intelligence about the defenders,
demoralize them through psychological warfare and covert
actions, pick off key commanders, provide the vanguard of
an attack using shock tactics, or even take out most of the
defenses on their own. They combined the functions of
burglars, commandos, spies, and assassins. Other strongholds, such as the palace of a *daimyo*, called for similar
skills, and in *ninjutsu* the discipline of "penetrating the
stronghold" was honed to a science.

Three main elements were involved in castle infiltration.
The *jin* (mankind) element made full use of psychology,
particularly in regard to the guards. Ninja would study
them and use their weaknesses, knowing what would
distract them, what they would ignore or fail to perceive,
when they were least alert, etc. The *chi* (earth) element involved finding the weak spots in the castle's defenses. This
might be a dimly lit area. Ninja often aimed for the highest part of the defenses; assuming that this was the most
difficult point at which to gain access, defenders would
leave these parts dark and unwatched. Another weak spot
would be one with many comings and goings, where the

guards would be distracted by diversions. Fires made useful diversions, and ninja were experts at using gunpowder to set and spread fires (see page 64). The ten elements involved choosing the correct time for infiltration.

Timing is Everything

In *ninjutsu,* there were said to be eight best times to attempt the ten elements:

1. **The night when a sick person in the stronghold (preferably the daimyo or other important person) was recovering from an illness.** This particularly applied to the mountain retreats where injured *daimyo* would hole up when they had been wounded in battle and needed to recover; these were usually at natural spa sites, and hence were known as "secret springs." This was the time when the *daimyo* were at their most vulnerable, so their personal retainers and bodyguards would probably be on maximum alert, only relaxing their guard when their master had recovered. Such a recovery might also be the occasion for a party—always a useful diversion for infiltration.

2. **After the defenders had enjoyed a heavy bout of drinking.** Too much sake provided opportunity for the ninja.

3. **When there had been a house fire nearby.** In the highly flammable and urban environment of medieval Japan, a fire nearby would also be a threat to the stronghold. The defenders might have been drawn off to lend a hand, or might simply be distracted by the commotion.

4. **During a celebration after refurnishing.** This sounds oddly specific, but it reflects the usefulness of a party as a diversion.

5. **If someone in the house had just died.** The defenders might be distracted by the death and the rituals associated with it.

6. **During a storm or heavy rain.** Reduced visibility, enhanced ambient noise levels, and distracting lightning and thunder provided useful cover for furtive climbing, sawing, digging, and so on, while guards were likely to be busier trying to keep warm and dry than keeping watch.

7. **At a time of commotion.** This is a fairly generic category—suggested causes for such a "commotion" might include a brawl between the defenders or the visit of a VIP.

8. **On a wedding night.** Again, the ceremony and subsequent partying were likely to distract the defenders and dull their wits.

GHOST TECHNIQUE

Ninja would use any sort of ruse to gain entry to a castle, if stealth and breaking and entering were not possible. They might use one of their traditional disguises (see page 100), or a less subtle approach. For instance, during the siege of Sawayama Castle in 1562, the ninja captain Igasaki Doshun and a mixed troop of Iga and Koga ninja gained entry using the simplest disguise imaginable: they simply copied the *mon* (family emblem or badge) of the defending forces and printed it on lanterns they carried. In this manner, they walked directly into the castle. The *Bansen Shukai* described this as an example of *bakemono-jutsu,* or "ghost technique." Another account from the same year of the siege of Kaminojo Castle records how a group of ninja disguised themselves in the same armor as the castle defenders.

DOG HANDLING

Fierce guard dogs were a common feature of defenses and security arrangements, and the ninja were trained to deal with these as well. One trick was to bring along a female dog in heat, which distracted a male guard dog. If this failed and the guard dog started barking, a simple ruse was to bark back, so that the defenders would simply assume it was reacting to another dog. If all else failed, the ninja could use his expertise in drugs and medicine to dope or poison the dog.

LIGHTS, FLAMES, ACTION

Getting into the stronghold was only half the job. Once ninja had infiltrated unobserved, they might hide in nooks, on rooftops, and in trees, in order to spy on the defenders, noting their numbers, condition, supplies, disposition, and routines. Alternatively, they might take advantage of disguises to mingle with the defenders and listen to their conversations. Once intelligence was gathered, the ninja had a number of options. They might pass the intelligence back to their own side, either by slipping out again, unnoticed, or by firing a message-bearing arrow back across the battle lines. They might talk to the defenders, spreading stories, stirring up discontent, and undermining morale. Or they might swing into action at an appointed moment (usually just before dawn), to carry out the first stage of a castle-storming attack.

Fire was a valuable weapon, given that many of the internal buildings, castle superstructures, and upper walls were constructed from wood, wattle-and-daub, thatch, and paper. Ninja would also attack the garrison, spreading fear, panic and confusion, especially if they were dressed like the defenders—the real guards would not know who to trust, and might fall upon one another.

ASSASSINATION

Today, the most popular image of the ninja is as a cat-burglar assassin who slips past any defense to reach his target. Historically, ninja did fulfill this role, and were in demand owing to the difficulty of reaching an enemy *daimyo*. *Daimyo* surrounded themselves with fanatically loyal cadres of samurai bodyguards, who rarely let them out of their sight, as they were suspicious at all times. Stephen Turnbull records that Takeda Shingen had two doors to his lavatory, so that he would always have an escape route in case of attack, and was of the opinion that a *daimyo* should ensure he had access to a dagger even when alone with his wife.

THE PERFECT HIT

The ideal ninja assassination operation brought together many of the tools and skills already outlined. Using climbing and breaking-and-entering tools, a ninja, or more likely a team of two ninjas, would scale the outer walls of the target's stronghold, perhaps with the help of an overhanging tree. Secreted in the garden they would watch and wait for their moment. When it came, they would steal silently towards the house and either climb onto the roof or crawl beneath the raised floor. From these vantage

points they could get an idea of the layout of the house and the position and movement of the guards, improving their field of vision by boring small holes using a tool such as the *shikoro*. Alternatively, ninja might already be equipped with inside information, possibly obtained from a *kunoichi* passing herself off as a servant.

Using tools such as the *kunai* or the *tsubokiri*, ninja would cut or force their way into an unoccupied chamber or corridor and move swiftly and silently towards the target, using the *yoko aruki* or *nuki ashi* walking techniques. If moving in the darkness, they might employ the extended *tsuba* technique. Once outside the target's room, they might cut a small hole and insert a *fukiya* (blowpipe) to fire poison-tipped darts, or they might opt for a strike through the paper wall if they knew the position of the target. Alternatively, they could burst in and use *shuriken*, swords, or *shinobi-gama* to take out both the target and any bodyguards.

To escape, the ninja would slow or stun pursuers using *arare*, *metsubushi*, or *hikyu*, and create cover for themselves using *torinoke*. With pursuit discouraged or deflected, the ninja could leave the same way they came in, making use of all their hiding, stealth, and disguise skills to lie low or avoid detection until they could return to their homes, their mission accomplished.

THE YOUTHFUL ASSASSIN

Few successful ninja assassinations are recorded, perhaps because the very best ones might be made to look like accidents or due to natural causes. Some Japanese historians list the first ninja assassination as the killing of Himma Saburo by a youth named Kumawaka sometime in the 1330s. Kumawaka had been sent as a hostage to the household of Saburo, who promptly had his father executed and cremated.

Swearing vengeance, Kumawaka bided his time for an opening. For five days he faked an illness, sneaking forth at night to gather intelligence on the layout of Saburo's house. He waited for a night of rain and high winds to act, creeping into Saburo's bedroom, where he planned to use his target's own sword to dispatch him. Worried that light from the lantern in Saburo's room would reflect off the blade of the sword and wake his prey, Kumawaka displayed typical ninja resourcefulness and creativity by dousing the light soundlessly. He opened one of the doors to the outside to allow in a host of moths, which quickly swamped the flame, extinguishing it. Protected now by the darkness, he drew the sleeping man's blade and ran him through. He then employed another typical ninja trick to escape, crossing the moat by climbing a tall bamboo stalk until it bowed beneath his wait, bending it over to deposit him on the far side of the water.

THE SPECIALISTS

By the Sengoku Jidai (Era of Warring States), true ninja assassins for hire had emerged onto the scene. Peculiarly, it seems that the most notable examples, in terms of who earned recognition in the chronicles, were thoroughly unsuccessful. For instance, the powerful *daimyo* Oda Nobunaga, who effectively brought an end to the Era of Warring States by unifying the country by ruthlessly crushing all of his enemies, generally relied on force of arms to achieve his aims, but was not above employing ninja assassins. He sent a ninja named Hachisuka Tenzo (probably an Iga ninja) to assassinate one of his arch-rivals, Takeda Shingen, but Tenzo bungled the job and narrowly escaped with his life.

Nobunaga himself was also apparently ninja-proof. There were multiple attempts on his life but none were successful. Legendary ninja Ishikawa Goemon is said to have made an attempt on his life (see page 172). He also survived an attempt on his life in 1571 by a sharpshooting Koga ninja named Sugitani Zenjubo. Another attempt failed during his suppression of the Iga ninja (see page 35), where three ninja fired a cannon at him but missed. Even the "shogun's ninja"—the Iga men in the service of Tokugawa Ieyasu—are recorded as having failed at an assassination attempt: a ninja named Kirigakure Saizo managed to infiltrate the stronghold of rival *daimyo* Toyotomi Hideyoshi, but didn't get past his floorboards before being flushed out.

NINJA ARCHITECTURE

The threat of ninja infiltration and assassination led canny *daimyo* to incorporate anti-ninja devices into the architecture of their homes. Similar devices might be found in the strongholds of ninja themselves, in case of an enemy attack.

VILLAGE PEOPLE

Indeed, the whole layout of a ninja village might be subtly geared towards defense despite appearing much like a normal farming community. A typical ninja village in the Iga hill country featured outlying watchposts with beacons to alert the villagers if danger threatened. A watchtower on the edge of the village served a similar function. The village itself was arranged around the home of the *shonin*, with apparently normal rice paddies, irrigation ditches, and field hedges and fences doubling as fields of fire, moats, and barriers that would slow attackers and force them to approach the central stronghold in narrow, vulnerable columns.

NINJA AND ANTI-NINJA HOMES

To make it difficult for an intruder to move around the home unnoticed, the corridors might have several modifications. One was a so-called "nightingale floor," a cleverly constructed design where the floorboards of the corridor were set atop very squeaky metal hinges or levers, such that it was impossible to place any weight on them without making considerable noise (likened to the singing of a nightingale, hence the name). Another clever modification was "ankle-breakers"—areas where the floorboards had been removed to reveal the joists beneath. An intruder walking along in the dark and unaware of their presence would fall between them. Sometimes pit-style booby traps lined with spikes were built below the floorboards. The Nijo-jinya house had a cunning set of stairs where the uprights were made of paper, allowing a guard hiding beneath the stairs to stab through at an intruder's legs and feet.

To protect the master of the house, any room in which he spent time, and particularly those in which he received visitors, would be flanked or overlooked by a room in which a guard could hide. Spy holes would allow the guard to watch proceedings, and if a threat became apparent he could drop into the room and surprise the assailant. The master himself might conceal a weapon behind a nearby fake panel or floorboard.

Other features would help the inhabitants escape, and delay or misdirect pursuers. Sliding panels might actually be hinged so as to rotate, giving access to previously hidden rooms or corridors. Secret doors and hidden stairways allowed people to "disappear," as did weighted false ceilings—with pressure applied to the right point these would swing down to reveal stairs or ladderways on the other side, and then swing back into place afterwards to give the appearance of a harmless ceiling. Such stairways might lead to concealed upper floors, with escape hatches onto the roof or outside.

忍 者

Even a sheet
of paper has
two sides.

—*Japanese Proverb*

The most pressing question for those who study the ninja is why the ninja have such a low profile in pre-Edo Japanese sources. The chronicles are full of references to teisatsu, rappa, and other terms, but they only rarely mention the characters for ninja / shinobi, and, crucially, they tend to do so in an ambiguous fashion.

Chapter 5
Ninja Culture and Controversies

A strong argument can be made that the ninja are more important culturally than historically. While the impact of the ninja in Japanese and world history has been uncertain and arguably minimal, its cultural impact has been significant and global in reach. Indeed, some contend that the ninja is almost entirely a cultural artifact, and that it has no existence outside this realm. This chapter explores this controversy, but first examines some of the cultural aspects of the ninja phenomenon, from the role of ninja as folk heroes and icons to the world of ninja-related media and entertainment.

TALES OF THE NINJA

It is possible to get a flavor of the true cultural impact and meaning of the ninja through tales of those who achieved distinction. The characters featured here often straddle the boundary between historical fact and folkloric fiction. Most or all of them may have been historical personages (who probably lived during the Sengoku period—the heyday of the ninja), but layers of legend,

myth, mysticism, and magic have accreted around their exploits. In this sense, they closely resemble parallel characters from Western culture, such as Robin Hood or King Arthur; figures who may have genuine historical foundations, but who are now viewed primarily through the prism of folklore and legend rather than history.

Whether or not they were true ninja, all reveal *shinobi* traits or employ *shinobi* skills or ruses. This has been enough for some writers to claim them as part of the ninja tradition, if indeed there is one.

PRINCE YAMATO

Said to have lived around the fourth century A.D. and to have been one of the sons of the 12th Emperor, this legendary prince of Japan is sometimes referred to as the first ninja, but is more properly described as a proto-ninja, or perhaps the first *shinobi* warrior (in the sense of being the first person recorded to have used *shinobi* tactics). Among the tales associated with him are two that particularly conform to this *shinobi* theme. The best known concerns an episode in which Yamato was sent to pacify the rebellious island of Kyushu. To infiltrate the court of the rebel chieftains, Yamato snuck into a banquet dressed as a maid-servant, letting his long tresses cascade down his back and concealing his sword beneath his dress. Fooled by the disguise, the ruling brothers invited him to sit between them. When they were distracted by the effects of the alcohol,

Yamato drew his sword, stabbing one of the brothers, and then chasing the other into the next room. Before the other brother was also killed, he bestowed upon Yamato the admiring epithet *takeru* (the brave).

In another episode, Yamatotakeru, as he is often known, was sent to impose control on the Izumo area, which in turn required that he beat the fearsome and renowned swordsman Izumo Takeru. Yamato cunningly had an exact wooden replica of his sword made, indistinguishable from the original, and then presented the actual sword to his unsuspecting foe. Impressed by the generous gift, Izumo extended the hand of friendship to the youngster. Later, after bathing together in a river, Yamato ensured that he was the first to get out of the water. Dressing quickly, he surreptitiously picked up the real sword and thrust it through his sash, leaving the wooden replica for Izumo. Unable to spot the difference, thanks to the cunning workmanship, Izumo donned the fake sword and was thus left defenseless when Yamato rather unsportingly challenged him to a duel and killed him.

Few historians consider these stories of Yamato to be reliable accounts of actual events. Even the very earliest, from the *Kojiki (Record of Ancient Events)*, the first known Japanese book, date from the early eighth century A.D., around 400 years after he was supposed to have lived. For ninja historians, however, it is considered significant that the oldest Japanese book discusses the

art of *shinobi*: already, it seems, it was recognized as an important attribute for a Japanese hero. It may also be significant that Yamato's tomb is located in Ise, in Iga (contemporary Mie Prefecture), today regarded as the ninja heartland.

HATTORI HANZO

Hanzo was probably the best known "true" ninja (in the sense that he is generally recognized to have been a leader of the Iga *shinobi no mono*). There may have been as many as four Hattori Hanzos who led the clan at one time or another, and this one was distinguished by his personal name Masanari (a.k.a., Masahige), and later by his nickname Oni no Hanzo, or Devil Hanzo. Hanzo was the son of Hattori Yasunaga, a minor samurai in the service of the Matsudaira clan (later to become the Tokugawa clan that would rule Japan in the Edo era), and was actually born in Mikawa, although he visited Iga frequently. Supposedly, he started his *ninjutsu* training at a prodigiously early age, fought his first battle at the age of sixteen, and was a full-fledged ninja master by the time he was eighteen.

Various magical and quasi-magical skills were attributed to him. For instance, he was said to be able to trans-locate; apparently he would sit, spread his fan, disappear behind it, and reappear in the next room. He was also said to be an expert at sensing the approach of a foe from behind, and he was renowned for his ability to seize and bind an opponent despite starting from a seated posture. Perhaps he was using the *sakki*-detection method supposedly practiced by modern Togakure-*ryu* disciples (see page 29). Hanzo is said even to have had psychic superpowers, such as psychokinesis (the ability to move things using only the power of the mind), precognition (the ability to see the future), and clairvoyance, which he used to sense remotely the movements and disposition of enemy forces.

The best-known story about Hattori Hanzo tells how he saved the life of future shogun Tokugawa Ieyasu when the latter found himself poorly protected and vulnerable in hostile territory after the murder of Oda Nobunaga. Hanzo led him to safety across Iga territory, protected by the ninja clans of the region (see page 36).

Not Drowning, but Cheating

A lesser known tale of Devil Hanzo is a classic example of a ninja fable. It may be purely apocryphal, but it illustrates how the use of *shinobi* techniques became a kind of folkloric motif for the Japanese. According to the tale, Hanzo and his master were rough-housing by a river when Ieyasu decided to test whether his retainer could match his own prodigious powers of breath-holding. Grabbing Hanzo and dragging him to the river, Ieyasu plunged them both beneath the water, but was dismayed to see the ninja effortlessly continuing to hold his breath

even as he himself struggled. Impressed, he asked about the limits of the ninja's underwater abilities, and was amazed when Hanzo claimed that he could hold his breath for days on end if required. To demonstrate, he jumped back into the river and disappeared from view. To the astonishment of the waiting onlookers, he did not appear for several hours, until an alarmed Ieyasu called out for him. A few moments later, Hanzo rose to the surface, not the slightest bit out of breath. When quizzed on how all this was possible, Hanzo explained the ruse. He simply dove out of view, swam a short way downriver, and came ashore, hiding behind a rock until he heard his name being called, whereupon he dove back in and reappeared at the spot where he had entered. This, Hanzo explained, was *ninjutsu*.

Ninja versus Ninja

A popular type of ninja tale concerns ninja-versus-ninja encounters. A classic example is the tale told of Hanzo's impersonation of Sarutobi Sasuke. Sarutobi was a famous ninja in his own right (see page 168), but had met a his death while attempting to spy on Tokugawa Ieyasu for his employer, who had lately been declared a rebel and who feared an attack. Hanzo was aware of Sarutobi's death, but was also aware that there might be back-up ninja in his retinue. Accordingly he arranged for the palace defenses to be relaxed just enough for another ninja, sent to check on Sarutobi, to gain entry. Hanzo himself then dressed in his ninja garb and impersonated the dead man, creeping around the castle and even disabling guards. Hanzo had also arranged for palace guards to discuss Sarutobi's (entirely fictitious) escape, and sure enough the back-up ninja overheard them. He was able to report back to his master that Sarutobi was alive and at-large in the Tokugawa palace, and that as a result Ieyasu would have his hands too full to turn his attention to punishing rebels. When Ieyasu duly launched his attack he thus caught his opponent unawares.

The Death of Hanzo

It was during another ninja-versus-ninja encounter, however, that Hanzo met his match and his end. The story goes that Ieyasu had commissioned Hanzo to hunt down and exterminate Fuma Kotaro, a famous ninja who had once been a respected retainer of the Hojo family (see below), but who was now, along with his men, reduced to piracy, and was proving particularly adept at striking Tokugawa possessions. Hanzo had a fleet of heavy gunboats constructed, each equipped with large cannon, intended to outgun Kotaro's lightweight fleet of lightly armed ships.

In 1596, cruising off the coast at Suo, Hanzo spotted a squadron of Kotaro's vessels and gave chase. His heavy guns soon knocked out most of the enemy ships, but a couple managed to keep out of range. He followed them into a narrow channel and appeared to have disabled and set one on fire. As the fight progressed, the tide changed and the current sucked Hanzo's fleet deeper into the channel, perilously close to the flaming ship and the threat it posed to their volatile powder magazines. Attempting to steer clear of danger, the Tokugawa fleet discovered that their rudders had been sabotaged, apparently by Fuma ninja using special underwater techniques. There was no time to dump the powder, so Hanzo ordered his men to abandon ship, only to discover that the sea was thick with oil. Kotaro's trap was now fully sprung, and the fireship collided with the Tokugawa fleet and set the oily seas ablaze, obliterating Hanzo and all his men.

This tale illustrates the common ninja-versus-ninja battle of *shinobi* tactics. Apparently, enough of Hanzo's remains were recovered to inter, as his tomb can today be found at the Sainen-ji temple cemetery in Shinjuku, Tokyo.

NAKAGAWA SHOSHUNJIN

Shoshunjin was a samurai who started the Nakagawa-*ryu* of *ninjutsu* in the mid-seventeenth century when he was tasked by his master, the *daimyo* Tsugaru Nobumasa, to teach *ninjutsu* to a small group of acolytes. Shoshunjin had twenty such followers, young samurai who were known as the *hayamichi no mono* (the short-cut people),

who secretly trained in *ninjutsu* in a closed-off corner of the castle, and were used for secret missions and espionage.

Stories told about Shoshunjin and his *ninjutsu* training include a variation on a common *ninjutsu* motif—the sword-theft. This is where a *ninjutsu* master proves his prowess by successfully meeting the challenge to steal a *daimyo's* sword, usually from beneath his very nose in his own sleeping quarters, possibly while he is actually holding onto it. In Shoshunjin's case, he was challenged by Tsugaru Gembin, as part of his "interview" process, to sneak in during the night and snatch Gembin's pillow from beneath his head. Resolving to get the better of this so-called *ninjutsu* expert, Gembin made sure that his head stayed firmly on his pillow, whatever the distraction. At one point, however, it began to rain outside, and Gembin suddenly felt drips falling onto his face. Thinking there must be a leak in the ceiling, he automatically raised his head to look for it, and when he lay back down his pillow had disappeared—into the hands of Nakagawa Shoshunjin, who had of course carefully arranged the diversionary "leak." Stephen Turnbull points out that this is probably not an authentic tale, since almost identical stories are told about a number of other ninja.

FUMA KOTARO

A bandit chief who worked for the Hojo clan, Fuma
(a.k.a., Kazama) Kotaro was a legendary figure sometimes portrayed as only partly human, with distinctly
ogre-like qualities. According to the martial chronicle
Hojo Godai-ki, he was a giant with upside-down eyes,
huge, brawny arms and legs, black whiskers, a wide
mouth with four projecting fangs, and a supernaturally
loud voice. In the chronicle he is called a *rappa*, a kind
of super-brigand, rather than a ninja. He was said to
combine the qualities of a sage and a thief. Later, he was
simply described as a ninja.

Among the famous exploits of Kotaro and his Fuma
ninja was the reduction of a Takeda force during the
1581 battle of Ukishimagahara. As with the Iga ninja's
harrying of Oda Nobuo's force (see page 106), Kotaro
played on the psychological aspect of guerrilla warfare
to reduce his opponents to nervous wrecks. For several
nights, whatever the conditions and irrespective of the
Takeda precautions, the Fuma ninja launched a series of
terrifying raids on the Takeda camp, snatching people,
panicking the horses, and setting fire to things, all the
while imitating the Takeda battle-cry so that the defenders could not tell friend from foe. Confusion reigned and
in their terror the Takeda forces turned on one another,
so that, in the morning, it became apparent that foot
soldiers had butchered their commanders and sons had
killed their own fathers. When a group of Takeda survi-

vors swore revenge, Kotaro was still too clever for them. Ten of them attempted to mingle with the Fuma forces as they were en route to another night attack. Kotaro forces had prearranged signals for sitting down and standing up; by using these secret signs, Kotaro soon found out who the interlopers were, and had them executed. Eventually the Tokugawa clan succeeded in subjugating the other great families and Kotaro was driven to piracy, claiming the scalp of Hattori Hanzo as one of his last great exploits.

THE SANADA TEN BRAVES

A legendary band of bodyguards, the Sanada Juyushi (Sanada Ten Braves, or the Ten Heroes of Sanada) were a group of ninja who fought under the semi-legendary samurai Sanada Yukimara during the siege of Osaka Castle in 1614–1615, the last gasp of the Sengoku era (see page 43). Yukimara was renowned as one of the greatest warriors of his age, but his clan was allied to a series of greater clans who fell afoul of the Nobunaga-Tokugawa axis, such as the Takeda, the Uesugi, the Hojo, and eventually the Toyotomi. Spared but exiled after Ieyasu's ascendancy to the Shogunate, Yukimara seized the opportunity of the Osaka showdown between the Toyotomi and the Tokugawa to return to the fray and make another attempt to kill his arch-enemy, the new Shogun. Besting vastly superior forces during both the winter and summer campaigns, Yukimara eventually

launched a direct attack on Ieyasu's forces despite being significantly outnumbered. Supposedly, the ferocity of his attacks brought him to within a few meters of the Tokugawa despot before he was finally killed, undone by exhaustion. During these epic battles he was said to have been assisted by a band of ten ninja: Sarutobi Sasuke (see below), Kakei Juzo (see below), Kirigakure Saizo, Miyoshi Sekai (or Miyoshi Seikai), Miyoshi Isa, Anayama Kosuke, Unno Rokuro, Nezu Jinpachi, Mochizuki Rokuro, and Yuri Kamanosuke.

SARUTOBI SASUKE

The best-known of the Sanada Ten Braves, Sasuke is now familiar to many Japanese as a character from children's fiction, and later from an eponymous comic book. His name is now almost synonymous with ninja characters in manga, anime, and computer-games.

Sarutobi means "monkey jump," alluding to his agility, speed, and prowess at leaping and climbing. It is said he could jump over or duck under the fastest blade. Legend has it that he was raised by monkeys. A story of his childhood relates how, at aged ten, he decided that his martial arts skills were too advanced for him still to be practicing with monkeys, so he set off to find a swordmaster. Arriving at Okunoin in the Torie Pass, the supreme sword-master Hakuunsai Tozawa took him as his pupil, and taught him the skills of fencing and *ninjutsu* for several years. This tale recalls similar accounts told of much earlier proto-ninja, such as Minamoto Yoshitsune, learning their arts from the *tengu*.

Sasuke's skills did not avail him during a reconnaissance mission in Tokugawa Ieyasu's stronghold, when he is said to have been caught in a bear trap as he attempted to leap out of the castle. He amputated his own foot to get free, but realized that he could not escape and committed ritual suicide (*seppuku*) instead.

KAKEI JUZO

Apart from having been one of the Sanada Ten Braves, Juzo is famous for tricking the Tokugawa clan into believing he was dead. Ieyasu had sent a ninja to deal with Juzo, but the pair proved to be old friends and Juzo enlisted his help. He pretended to have been captured by the Tokugawa ninja, and was brought before Ieyasu, who granted him the honor of death by *seppuku*. Everyone present clearly saw him plunge his dagger into his belly, from which blood duly spurted. The "corpse" was tossed into the castle moat, where it later reanimated and escaped unnoticed—the ruse had been perpetrated with the help of a dead fox, concealed beneath Juzo's jacket, into which he had plunged the knife. Juzo went on to harass Tokugawa forces for some time to come, now aided by the fact that his enemies thought him dead.

TOBI KATO

Tobi (Flying) Kato was famous for his presumed magical powers. Originally, he was called Kato Danzo. He acquired his more popular name when he tried to break into a house, but got wind of the fact that the occupiers and their guards were waiting for him. Using his *shinobifuku* he quickly fashioned a dummy and tied a rope to it before flinging it over the wall into the garden. Mistaking it for the real thing, the guards loosed a volley of arrows. When Danzo immediately pulled the dummy back over the wall, they were astonished to see that he had apparently changed direction in mid-air and leaped in the other direction, as though he could fly.

Danzo practiced a variety of other tricks. In one illusion he apparently made a bull disappear. In another he planted two leaves from a bush into the ground and made them sprout into an entire bottle-gourd tree, from which he then proceeded to cut a gourd. Hearing of his trickery, the *daimyo* Uesugi Kenshin resolved to hire him as a ninja, but first put him to the weapon-stealing test, demanding that Danzo steal a *naginata* (halberd) from the bedside of one of his retainers, Naoe Kanetsugu. To accomplish this Danzo had to scale high walls, leap across a moat, and deal with a fierce guard dog, which he poisoned with spiked rice. Not only did he carry off the *naginata*, as promised, he also took a young servant girl for good measure.

There is a saying that a skillful ninja cannot be loved by his master, and in Danzo's case it seems that he may have been too skillful. While he was in the service of Kenshin, Kanetsugu plotted to kill him, and when he took refuge in service with Kenshin's rival Takeda Shingen he was suspected of being a double-agent and put to death.

ISHIKAWA GOEMON

Goemon was a legendary sixteenth century bandit, and he is the perfect illustration of the evolution of the ninja as a cultural artifact. When he first appears in recorded history—for instance, an early mention is in a biography of Toyotomi Hideyoshi, written in 1642—he is simply referred to as a bandit. As his legend became more popular and tales of his anti-authoritarian exploits and cunning tricks proliferated, he was labeled a ninja, despite the lack of historical or documentary authority for this attribution. Goemon became one of the early ninja superstars thanks to his popularity as a subject for Kabuki and *bunraku* (puppet) theater, appearing in such Kabuki blockbusters as *Romon Gosan-no kiri* (the famous *Forty-Seven Ronin*), first staged in 1778.

Among the exploits attributed to Goemon, apart from his generous habit of robbing from the rich to give to the poor, was his attempt to assassinate Oda Nobunaga by sneaking into the ceiling space above Nobunaga's bed and trying to drip poison down a thread into his target's

mouth. The best-known tale about Goemon, however, is that of his attempt in 1594 to assassinate Toyotomi Hideyoshi, which was thwarted when he accidentally woke the *daimyo* by knocking a bell off a table. He was sentenced to be boiled in oil along with his infant son, but proved his nobility of spirit by holding his son clear of the boiling oil even as he perished.

THE NINJA IN JAPANESE AND WESTERN CULTURE

The Sengoku, or Warring States, period saw the heyday of the historical ninja, but just a few decades later the ninja had become transformed into a cultural, rather

than military-political, phenomenon. The ascendancy of the Tokugawa clan ushered in the Edo Period, an era of oppression and authoritarianism. There was military and political stability, but this could not prevent social change, and the dynamic energies of the changing society found expression through culture, and specifically through what came to be known as the *ukiyo*, or "floating world." The floating world was a sort of cultural movement focused on pleasure and entertainment, and both met and created an accelerating demand for cultural content, with an explosion of chronicles, novels, woodblock prints, music, and theater.

FACT TO FANTASY

By the mid-seventeenth century, ninja began to feature in this expanding artistic output, with tales of famous samurai and romantic brigands who demonstrated *shinobi* techniques and virtues. Gradually, these figures became folkloric ninja, accreting the ninja's mystical and magical attributes along the way, including invisibility, flight, and even the power to transform into animals. Tales of Nakagawa Shoshunjin, for instance, described his ability to turn into a bird, while popular kabuki plays involved ninja magicians turning into toads, rats, and spiders.

Later, this trend for the fantastical aspect of *ninjutsu* went to strange and even absurd lengths, especially in terms of the technology and gadgetry ninja were said to possess. They were said to have used tanks (in the form of tortoise-shell wagons), submarines, and other aquatic gear; Ferris-wheel-like siege-engines that delivered ninja to the ramparts of besieged castles; and wrecking-ball cranes for knocking down the walls. Legend has it that they also developed early forms of aerial bombardment, using kites and hang-gliders from which to drop bombs, and that they even used catapults to hurl ninja over the heads of the enemy so that they could drop their grenades mid-flight and then open parachutes in order to drift back down to earth. Perhaps the most absurd device yet suggested is one dreamt up by Masaaki Hatsumi, who posits what Stephen Turnbull describes as a "bovine flamethrower"—a hollow wooden cow on wheels, containing a ninja who operates a flame-spewing device from within.

NINJA ICONOGRAPHY

By the early nineteenth century the iconography of the ninja began to evolve into what we know today. The first known image of a classic black-clad ninja is found in an illustrated book of 1802 and shows a ninja climbing across a moat to gain entry to a castle, using a classic ninja grapnel-and-rope device. Subsequently, both assassins and heroes (such as the Forty-Seven Ronin) were depicted in ninja garb. Perhaps the emergence of such depictions was linked to the developing association between the *kurogo* stage-hands of Kabuki and *bunraku*

theater and the costume of ninja characters in the plays (see page 57).

At the same time a parallel strand of ninja iconography was emerging—the depiction of the ninja as rapists. Several books and woodblock print collections of the period feature ninja raping both willing and unwilling victims, putting their talents of breaking and entering, stealth, and rope-tying to evil use. This link between ninja, eroticism, and sadism persisted well into the twentieth century.

Ninja Crazes

Ninja continued to be a popular subject for Japanese arts and literature into the early twentieth century. Sarutobi Sasuke, for instance, was a popular character in children's literature between 1911 and 1925. But to understand the modern ubiquity of the ninja as a cultural archetype on a par with cowboys or pirates, it is necessary to look to the ninja "crazes" of the 1960s and 1980s, which gripped Japan and firmly implanted the ninja "meme" in the consciousness of the West.

After World War II, the Japanese tradition of woodblock printing and illustrated fiction matured into what is now widely known as manga—Japanese comic book art—and the ninja became a popular subject for best-selling manga. A classic example is the 1962 manga *Sarutobi Sasuke*, by Sampei Shirato. Manga in turn fed into Japanese film and

television, and later *anime* (Japanese animation) and computer games, all of which commonly feature ninja characters, who often bear the names of historical ninja.

The work of Sampei Shirato and others like him began the ninja craze of the 1960s, which soon percolated into film. In 1962, The film *Shinobi No Mono* was released—it was a historical fantasy based on the life of legendary bandit ninja Ishikawa Goemon. This was a huge hit in Japan and triggered a wave of "ninja-sploitation" films, the quantity of which far outweighed the quality. The craze collapsed under the weight of its own mediocrity within a few years. *Shinobi No Mono* itself spawned no less than six sequels, three of which were rushed out within a year of the original. This series was also notable because it employed the services of Masaaki Hatsumi as a technical advisor. This job was part of his long and fruitful career in television and film, which included advising and appearing in dozens of films and shows. Hatsumi even had his own show at one point, *Ninja Olympiad*. He was so renowned that on one occasion he was requested to present a lecture to the Emperor himself.

INTO THE WEST

One major consequence of the ninja craze of the early 1960s was that it caught the eye of Ian Fleming, creator of James Bond, who was in Japan to research his next

Bond novel, *You Only Live Twice*. When the novel (1964) and its film version (1967) came out, they duly featured armies of black-clad ninja, ingenious ninja technology and *ninjutsu* skills, and a classic ninja assassination attempt where poison is dripped down a thread. Thanks to the success of the movie, the ninja became lodged in Western consciousness, both in fiction and fact. One result of the new Western interest in *ninjutsu* was that Westerners started to seek out *ninjutsu* masters such as Hatsumi, training with them and bringing *ninjutsu* back to their own countries.

However, ninja-mania did not fully take hold in the West until 1981, with the release of *Enter the Ninja*, a Menahem Golen movie that was an enormous global success. It made a star of its Japanese anti-hero, Sho Kosugi, and triggered a wave of Western ninja-sploitation movies to match Japan's efforts of the early 1960s.

TURTLES

Most significantly, the ninja craze of the 1980s inspired American comics to start featuring ninja, which led in turn to two young American comic book artists producing a spoof entitled *Teenage Mutant Ninja Turtles*. When it first appeared in 1984, the comic was a cult hit restricted to a few knowledgeable, and mainly adult, comics fans, but in 1987 Ninja Turtle-mania exploded worldwide, thanks to an animated television series for

children, accompanied by a tidal wave of merchandise. Owing to the Turtles phenomenon, many aspects of ninja lore became virtually ubiquitous in world youth culture.

THE INVERSE NINJA LAW

In popular culture, it appears that the potency of ninja characters is in inverse proportion to their numbers. In other words, the more ninja there are, the less effective they seem to become. As a cultural archetype, the lone ninja signifies certain qualities—most notably, that he is a one-man killing machine of incredible prowess and resourcefulness, who can penetrate any defense, enter any stronghold, and defeat practically any number of opponents. In stories where a group of heroes encounter a lone ninja, they usually suffer at least a temporary defeat despite their numerical superiority.

As the number of ninja increases, however, something strange happens to their skills, especially with regard to their interaction with the heroes. When hoards of ninja attack a hero or heroes, they are transformed into mere cannon-fodder, apparently unable to hit a target with their *shuriken* from even a few feet, and incapable of defeating vastly outnumbered opponents. Obviously, this is the result of narrative demands (i.e., the story would be

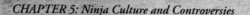

over quickly if the hero was simply massacred), but the effect is to somewhat dispel the aura of super-powers and magic that the ninja acquired in his earlier, Edo-Period fictional incarnations.

THE NINJA CONTROVERSY

Reflections on the cultural characteristics of the ninja phenomenon lead us back to a common motif of discussions of the ninja—namely, that they often appear to

have greater fictional than historical presence. The question of the ninja's historical presence is controversial, and no book on the ninja would be complete without a serious consideration of the issue.

KEEPING A LOW PROFILE

The most pressing question for those who study the ninja is why the ninja have such a low profile in pre-Edo Japanese sources. The chronicles are full of references to *teisatsu*, *rappa*, and other terms, but they only rarely mention the characters for ninja and *shinobi*, and, crucially, they tend to do so in an ambiguous fashion. They use the terms fairly generically, in the same way that European chroniclers might have used the words "spy" or "assassin," rather than appearing definitively to refer to a specifically initiated cadre or secret society of specifically constituted ninja. Most of the historical or folkloric characters who today are routinely described as ninja originally had quite different occupations attributed to them. For instance, Hattori Hanzo and Nakagawa Shoshunjin were both referred to as samurai, while Fuma Kotaro and Ishikawa Goemon were said to have been brigands or bandits. Why do ninja, in the modern understanding of the word, seem to be missing from Japanese history?

Various explanations have been advanced to account for the scarcity of historical reference to the ninja. Some *ninjutsu* masters point out that the very nature of their craft means that it would have remained hidden and unrecorded. In his book *Tiger Scrolls of the Koga Ninja*, Jay Sensei explains, "The laws of the Ninjas [sic] forbade them to tell anyone that they were Ninjas . . . Should they break these laws and reveal the Secrets of Ninjutsu, they would be killed by their own group." Masaaki Hatsumi, perhaps the foremost modern practitioner and promoter of *ninjutsu*, makes the same point even more succinctly: "If one did know the truth about *ninjutsu*, it would no longer be true *ninjutsu*."

Other writers point out that history is written by the dominant forces in society, which in Japan meant the samurai classes, the natural antagonists of the ninja. They may well have been inclined to airbrush the dishonorable deeds of the despised *shinobi no mono* from the pages of Japan's story. But the third, highly controversial explanation is that the ninja did not really exist, and that they have been retrospectively constituted by latter day myth-makers cobbling together scattered historical references to spies, assassins, scouts, and commando forces.

THE CASE AGAINST THE NINJA

According to this school of thought, ninja scholars have systematically over-interpreted the references to *shinobi* and other terms to create a society or profession that did not really exist. This would explain the diversity of terms used to characterize these bandits, brigands, scouts, secret agents, and covert warriors. Rather than being the secret art of the ninja clans, taught only to the initiated, *ninjutsu* was a loosely-defined and widely varying body of knowledge and techniques that any warrior could learn, just as any medieval European warrior could have learned to be a spy, scout, or commando-style soldier.

What about the association of the Iga and Koga regions with the ninja? It may be that the Iga and Koga regions, for geographical, social, and historical reasons, particularly encouraged the development of unconventional warfare and warriors, just as some mountainous regions in other parts of the world, such as Switzerland or Afghanistan, have traditionally been associated with independently-minded, tough, resourceful, guerrilla fighters. But this is not the same as saying that they were home to specific ninja societies. The Iga and Koga men employed by Tokugawa Ieyasu and his successors may have been retrospectively labeled as ninja, when in fact they were simply skilled at *shinobi* arts.

According to ninja skeptics, many other facets of ninja lore and history were also fashioned retrospectively. The original sources for most of this ninja lore are ninja "handbooks" such as the *Bansen Shukai*, none of which predate the Edo period. The ninja-skeptic suggestion is that these were at least partly fictional, created for entertainment rather than education. This would explain apparently farfetched or ridiculous items such as the water-spiders (see page 75) or the cat's-eye clock (see page 99).

WORKING-CLASS HERO?

If the ninja skeptics are correct, and the ninja as they are generally understood today did not really exist, how can we account for the evolution of this cultural archetype, its endurance, and its abiding popularity? One explanation is that the ninja should be viewed as a manifestation of an even older and more universal archetype: the trickster. The trickster is a form of cultural hero found in the myths, legends, and folklore of every society and culture in history and around the world. He uses tricks and ruses to outwit the strong and the powerful—the establishment—and to assert the power of the individual. Often he acts in decidedly non-heroic fashion to accomplish these ends: he is not a hero in the moral or virtuous sense.

If this character sounds familiar in the context of the ninja, it is surely no coincidence. In a society as rigidly stratified, conformist, and anti-individualistic as Japan (and particularly the Japan of the Edo period), the appeal, even the necessity, of such an archetype becomes obvious. The use of *shinobi* techniques by ninja characters and their forebears (such as Prince Yamato) is a way of challenging and subverting the traditional Japanese virtues such as manliness, open combat, force of arms and death before dishonor. By contrast with these virtues, we see ninja characters dressing as women, using stealth to secretly infiltrate strongholds, killing from the shadows, pretending to be other people, using poisons, etc. A parallel part of the ninja myth is that *ninjutsu* developed as a sort of working-class or peasants' alternative to the *bushido* of the samurai (see page 14). This is very much in keeping with the concept of the ninja as an anti-establishment trickster cultural hero. In summary, perhaps it is the correspondence between the ninja and the trickster archetype that accounts for his cultural resonance, his origin, and his enduring popularity.

Ninja is as Ninja Does

The ninja skeptic view and its cultural rationale may not satisfy everyone. There are many ninja enthusiasts and believers who do not accept that the ninja simply might be a fiction. Some observe that modern ninja define themselves, through their practice and mastery of *ninjutsu*, and not through any supposed descent from historical schools of ninja. In other words, whether or

not ninja existed centuries ago, they unquestionably exist today. Ninjutsu master and ninja historian Roy Ron
sums up this view:

"It is compelling to recognize as Ninja those, including ourselves, who learn, practice, teach and preserve
these martial traditions [of *ninjutsu*]. But if the historical
Ninja no longer exist, we are left with the same dilemma
of self-identity. The solution to that dilemma lies in
recognizing that we need to look at the essence of these
martial traditions, not at their historical context. That
is, these martial traditions [. . .] transmit a world-view,
philosophy and fighting spirit that are not bound by
historical periods. Therefore, it is more accurate to view
the historical Ninja as having been replaced by modern
warriors who preserve pre-modern fighting traditions.
Whether this qualifies one as a Ninja [. . .] is a matter
of self-perception, not of historical continuation."

Epilogue

It is perhaps the crowning achievement of the ninja art that debate still rages today about their very existence. Generations of these shadow warriors have dedicated their lives to perfecting subterfuge and stealth, and so what greater compliment can we give to these masters of trickery than to doubt their very existence?

The two kanji characters that make up the word "ninja" combine the ideas of "quiet action" and "one who endures." Although the latter attribute refers to the ninja's dogged pursuit of a goal, it is also true that the legend of the ninja endures, and will no doubt persist for centuries to come.

Roy Ron stresses that whether the ninja legacy lives on is a matter of self-perception rather than historical continuation. Indeed, any flexible system that continued the ninja ethos would by definition be grounded in the present and the future in favor of harking back to the past, no matter how iconic. In the words of pre-eminent modern teacher and promoter of ninjutsu, Masaaki Hatsumi, "focus on the future for fifty percent, on the present for forty percent, and on the past for ten percent."

Masaaki Hatsumi also gives the enigmatic, humorous, and beguiling advice: "Only teach fifty percent of what you know." It is tempting to interpret a comment such as this from a modern *ninjutsu* master as a hint that the secrets of the ninja continue to be passed on in secret to a select few, while mainstream martial arts has to content itself with a fraction of this body of knowledge. Though their image was the unglamorous inverse of the noble and aristocratic samurai, the ninja and the tradition of making the ninja appear larger than life has enjoyed a very long history indeed, and is still very much alive.

Glossary

akindo merchants/traders

akuryoku gripping training

amegasa sedge hat

arare caltrops

ashi running exercises

ashiko spikes worn on the feet

boshi ken thumb-drive fist, made by curling the knuckles so that the second joint of the fingers projects

bunraku puppet theatre

caltrops tetrahedral pointed devices that always have one point aiming upward

chiren knowledge training

chunin in the ninja hierarchy, those in charge of operations

daimyo feudal lords

daken taijutsu art of attacking the bones with strikes, kicks, and blocks

fudo ken clenched-fist position with fingers bent at the knuckles

fukibari spitting needs from the mouth or a blowpipe

fukiya blowpipe

futari jinba two-man jumping technique used to launch a ninja over a wall

gakushi musician or strolling player

gando specialized lantern

genin ninja foot soldiers

geta wooden sandals with projecting slats

gyaku climbing feat in which the ninja lies at full length, upside-down, on the ceiling

henso hoko jutsu drunken stagger used by ninja as a disguise

hidake short lengths of bamboo filled with gunpowder

hijo gunpowder-filled ball of paper with a sharp stick stuck through it to be thrown like a dart

hikyu fire balls

hira no kamae receiving posture that allows ninja to block punches and kicks

hiya gunpowder filled tubes attached to an arrow

hokode finger claws

ichimonji no kamae defensive posture

inro medicine carrier

irogome colored rice code

jishaku magnet used as a compass

ju taijutsu ninja fighting method that involves grappling and throwing

jumonji no kamae offensive posture that the ninja uses to launch attacking moves

kaginawa hooked rope

kaiki opening tools

kakejin exercise in which the ninja trainee hangs from a branch for hours while weighted with sacks of stones

kaki fire tools

kakute finger ring with a spike or hook that could be used to strike a deadly blow

kamae body posture or stance for unarmed combat

kancho spies

kasugai hand-held crampons

katana sword

keika espionage strategy in which captured ninja reinforce misinformation

kettsuin ritual magic finger movements

kisho surprise attackers

ko ashi walking with small, stabbing steps

komuso mendicant flute-playing monks

koran agitators

kunai trowel-like gouging device

kunoichi female ninja

kurogo prop-handler in Kabuki theatre

kurorokagi ice-axe-like devices

kusari-gama chain-and-sickle weapon

ma ai fighting method in which where the ninja uses close-in moves against a fighter who specializes in distance moves

manga Japanese comic book art

metsubushi twists or bags of paper filled with sand, pepper, and metal shavings and thrown at an opponent's eyes

mitsumono spies

mizugumo flotation devices that allow a ninja to walk on water

mizukakigeta flipper-like footwear for swimming

mon family emblem or badge

mudo practiced stillness for the ninja lying-in-wait

mudra hand gestures

musubi art of knots and tying people up

naginata halberd

nekkote a type of finger claw

nekome telling time by observing dilation of a cat's pupils

netane espionage tactic of planting agents in situations months to years in advance

ninjutsu the skills and techniques practiced by ninja

noboriki climbing tools

nokizaru "rooftop monkeys"; commandoes

nuki ashi sweeping step

ongyo methods used by ninjas for concealment

oniwaban secret service position for ninja serving the shogun

onmitsu spy or detective

rappa brigand

ronin masterless, unaffiliated samurai

ryu school or clan

sageo cord

sakki "the force of a killer"; a psychic emanation of malice

sannin jinba three-man jumping technique used to launch a ninja over a wall

saoto hikigane listening device similar to an ear trumpet

sarugaku dancers and entertainers

saya scabbard

seki hitsu "stone brush," a sort of writing kit

Sengoku Jida Era of Warring States

seppuku ritual suicide

shikan ken extended knuckle fist for striking an breakable bones

shikoro saw with a triangular blade

shimeki iron bars with wedged ends used to jam doors

shinobi kumade collapsible sectioned bamboo device that the ninja used to put a rope or hook over the wall

shinobi no mono a person skilled in the art of stealth

shinobi stealth, endurance

shinobibune collapsible lightweight boat

shinobifuku traditional ninja costume

shinobi-gama weighted chain-and-sickle weapon

shinobigatana ninja's sword

shinobijo bamboo staff with a fold out knife at one end and hollow compartment for poison darts at the other

shinobikagi collapsible bamboo-and-rope stepladder

shinobitsue bamboo staff used a type of ladder

shinren heart training

shizen no kamae nautral standing posture for the fighting ninja

shobo a wooden ring with a small projecting wedge that can be used to target pressure points

shogun ruler of Japan (as regent or commander-in-chief for Emperor)

shonin head of ninja clan

shukke Buddhist priests or monks

shuriken throwing blade or star

shuto sword hand

suiki water tools

sunamochi strengthening exercise involving holding clay pots filled with sand at arm's length

suntetsu a small oval piece of wood fixed to the finger with a strap

tabi two-toed sock-shoes with a gap between the big toe and the rest of the toes

tabidatsu "setting out"; first phase of a ninja operation

taibumi travel bow

tairen body training

takezutsu breathing pipe

teisatsu scouts

tekagi hand claws outfitted with spines or hooks, used in fighting to punch, slap, or parry

tengu fierce bird-demons of Japanese folklore

tobibashigo throwing ladder

tobu jumping training

togime door-jamming device

torinoke birds' eggs; blown eggs filled with gunpowder

tsuba sword-guard

tsubokiri gouging and wedging device

uchitake a bamboo tube used as a waterproof container

ukidaru flotation device

ukiyo "floating world"; a cultural movement focused on pleasure and entertainment

waraji straw sandals

yamabushi mountain warrior-priests

yoko aruki sideways walking

yoroi armor

zukin cowl

Bibliography

Adams, Andrew. *The Invisible Assassins*. Ohara Publications, 1980.

Cooper, Christian. *Chris' Ninja Page*. http://glass.tvu.ac.uk/~chi/ninja/ninja.html, accessed 11/25/06.

Draeger, Donn F. *Ninjutsu: The Art of Invisibility*. Tuttle Library of Martial Arts, 1992.

Hayes, Stephen K. *Ninja and Their Secret Fighting Art*. Charles E. Tuttle Co, 1981.

Hayes, Stephen K. *Quest Center*. www.skhquest.com, accessed 11/13/06.

Kim, Ashida. *Secrets of the Ninja*. Paladin Press, 1981.

Masaaki, Hatsumi. The *Warrior Information Website*. www.winjutsu.com, accessed 12/6/06.

Masaaki, Hatsumi. *The Way of the Ninja: Secret Techniques.* Kodansha International, 2004.

Nepstad, Peter. *The Illuminated Lantern.* www.illuminatedlantern.com/cinema/index.shtml, accessed 12/19/06.

Oda, Hirohisa. *Real Ninja.* Ninja Publishing, 2002.

Ron, Roy. *Genbukan Tokyo Shibu.* www.ninpo.org, accessed 11/1/06.

Ronson, Jon. *The Men Who Stare at Goats.* Picador, 2004.

Sensei, Jay. *Tiger Scrolls of the Koga Ninja.* Paul H Crompton Ltd, 1984.

Turnbull, Stephen. *Ninja: A.D. 1460-1650.* Osprey Publishing, 2003.

Turnbull, Stephen. *Ninja: The True Story of Japan's Secret Warrior Cult.* Caxton Editions, 1991.

Weiss, Al and Philbin, Tom. *Ninja: Clan of Death.* Pocket, 1981.

Index